THE
FIRST-TIME
MANAGER

THE
FIRST-TIME
MANAGER

A PRACTICAL GUIDE
TO THE MANAGEMENT OF PEOPLE

LOREN B. BELKER

A DIVISION OF AMERICAN MANAGEMENT ASSOCIATIONS

Library of Congress Cataloging in Publication Data

Belker, Loren B
   The first-time manager.

   1. Management.   2. Office management.
I. Title.
HD31.B3778   658.4   78-12993
ISBN 0-8144-5492-5

Seventh Printing

*Dedicated to
Darlene, Jeff, and Kay,
who knew it could be done,
and to my late brother Edward,
for his courageous inspiration.*

Acknowledgments

There are always people who interact on our lives and often have a greater impact than they're aware of at the time.

First and foremost is my family, who encouraged me at every turn over the long months involved in writing this book. Their sacrifices certainly exceeded any I may have made.

I wish to thank Professor Bill Torrence, from the Department of Management at the University of Nebraska, who read an early draft and offered encouragement at a time it was deeply needed.

Also, my thanks go to insurance executive Barbara Lautzenheiser, F.S.A., who allowed me to try out some of my ideas on her multitalented intellect.

And special thanks for their enthusiasm and professional skill go at last to Betty Cobb, who typed some of the early manuscript, and Debbie Fisk, who completed the manuscript preparation.

Contents

Introduction

So you're going to manage people. Your life will never be the same.

You're embarking on a stage of your career that will be an unending challenge. That challenge will be the achievement of goals or objectives through others. That is what supervision and management are all about.

Although this book is written primarily from an office management point of view, the application of these principles should be beneficial to anyone who is about to embark on a managerial career. Our relationship with other human beings is the most challenging opportunity that exists for us. It covers all aspects of our lives.

There are many books on the subject of management, but very few of them address themselves to—or zero in on—the individual who is about to begin a career of leading others. These persons are not interested in a lot of academic claptrap, but are rather in a state of mixed emotions—absolutely delighted with the promotion and absolutely panic-stricken with the realization that from now on they'll be judged by how well their subordinates perform.

1

This book is for those people, not for top management with thirty years' experience, even though many top managers would do well to refresh their acquaintanceship with some of the basic principles that will be discussed.

I've attempted to write this guide in a conversational manner, much as if I were talking to you. I trust you'll find it easy to refer back to specific areas should problems arise in the future. I strongly recommend that you reread this book after six months' experience of leading other people. Some of the concepts may take on additional usefulness at that time.

Thanks for deciding to spend some time with me.

I

The new kid on the block

1

How people are chosen for supervision

Unfortunately, many companies don't go through a very thorough process in choosing those who are to be moved into managerial positions. Often the judgment is based solely on how well the person is performing in the currently assigned task. The best performer doesn't always make the best manager, although many companies still make the choice on that basis. The theory is that successful past performance is the best indicator of future success.

It's important that you have a record of being successful, but being the best operator doesn't make you the best leader for a number of reasons. If the current job doesn't require that you work cooperatively with others, you could be performing well as a loner.

So the fact that you're a good performer, even though it demonstrates a success pattern, doesn't necessarily mean you'll be successful as a manager. Being a manager requires skills beyond those of being a satisfactory operator.

Some companies have management training programs. These vary from excellent to horrible. Too often the program is given to people who have already been in managerial positions for a number of years. If the program has any merit, it should be given to individuals who are being considered for management positions. This helps them avoid mistakes and also gives the trainee the opportunity to see whether he or she will be comfortable leading others. Anyone who has worked for any length of time has observed situations where promotions didn't work out and the person asked for the old job back. There's an old cliché that states, "Don't wish too hard for something because you might get it." Some people become so concerned with the gratification of a promotion, with its additional salary, that they don't spend enough time doing a self-analysis about whether they'll be suited for the change in responsibilities.

The Octopus

There are those who really believe that if you want something done right, you'd better do it yourself. People with this attitude rarely make good leaders because they have difficulty delegating responsibility. We've all seen them: they delegate only those trivial tasks that any idiot could perform, and anything meaningful they keep themselves. As a result, they work evenings and weekends and take a briefcase home as well. I'm not putting down overtime, because all of us occasionally must devote some extra time to the job, but people who follow this pattern as a way of life are poor managers. They have so little faith in their subordinates that they trust them with nothing important. What they're really saying is that they don't know how to properly train their people.

There's usually a turnover problem in a section with this kind of manager. The employees are usually more qualified than the "octopus" believes (the term "octopus" is used because such a leader reaches out and takes personal possession of all the responsible tasks) and they soon tire of handling only trivia.

I suspect you know of an "octopus" in your own office. I hope you're not working for one, because you'll have a difficult time being promoted. Caught up in your impossible situation, you're not given anything responsible to do, and as a result you never get a chance to demonstrate what you can do. You seldom get a recommendation for promotion from "Mr. Octopus"—assuming for a moment that he's a man. He's convinced that the reason he has to do all the work is because his people don't accept responsibility. He can never admit that it's because he refuses to delegate.

"Mr. Octopus" is a tragedy and should never have been put into a responsible position. When he himself gets passed over for promotion, he becomes quite bitter because no one works harder than he does, and obviously his efforts are not appreciated.

Particular attention has been given to "Mr. Octopus," primarily so that you won't allow yourself to fall into this trap. If you do become this kind of monster, it probably follows on your having just received your last promotion up the corporate ladder—unless the top exec is an "octopus" himself. In that case the whole organization is in trouble, and there's a good chance the top exec will die a premature death. We've all known people like that, too.

One other unvarying trait of a "Mr. Octopus" is that he seldom takes his vacation all at once. He takes it a couple of days at a time because the company obviously can't continue functioning without him any longer than that. I've known "octopus" leaders whose retirement years were absolutely demolished because retirement meant abolition of their reason for living, their dedication to the job.

The Chosen Few

In many organizations, new managers are chosen because of the current supervisor's recommendation. If you're fortunate, you're working for such a person. This type of leader gives subordinates a great deal of latitude; as a result, the department achieves a reputation as a breeding ground for future managerial talent. (We'll talk more in a subsequent chapter about how you can develop into this kind of manager.)

People are also chosen to head a function because they're related to the boss. Consider yourself fortunate if you're not in such a company. Even if you *are* related to the boss, it's very difficult to assume additional responsibility under such circumstances. You doubtless have the authority, but today's businesses aren't dictatorships and people won't perform well for you just because you've been anointed from on high. So, if you're the boss's son, you really have to prove yourself. You'll get surface respect, but let's face it—it's what people really think of you, not what they say to you, that matters and that affects how they perform. If you're the boss's son, you might consider getting your experience elsewhere before taking on a supervisory position in your dad's firm. Since the vast majority of you are not in that position, let's see what other problems you face.

In most organizations, you're not chosen for a managerial position because of your technical knowledge. You're chosen because someone has seen the spark of leadership in you. That's the spark you must start developing. Leadership is difficult to define. A leader is a person others look to for direction, a person whose judgment is respected because it's usually sound. As you exercise your judgment and develop the capacity to make sound decisions, it becomes a self-perpetuating characteristic. Your faith in your own decision-making power is fortified. That feeds your self-confidence, and with more self-confidence you become less reluctant to make difficult decisions.

A leader is a person who can see into the future and visualize the result of his or her decision making. A leader is also a person who can set aside matters of personality and make decisions based on fact. This doesn't mean you ignore the human element—you never ignore it, but you deal always with the facts themselves, not with people's emotional perception of those facts.

People are chosen to be managers for a wide variety of reasons. If you're chosen for sound reasons, your acceptance by your new subordinates will, for the most part, be much easier to come by.

2

The first few months

Your first week on the job as a manager will be unusual, to say the least. If you're a student of human behavior, you'll observe some surprising developments.

Settling In

Don't believe that everyone is happy about the choice of the new kid on the block. Some of your co-workers will feel *they* should have been chosen. They may be jealous of your new promotion and secretly hope you fall on your face.

Others, the office "yes people" will immediately start playing up to you. As the chosen one, you can be their ticket to success. Their objective isn't all bad, but their method of operation leaves something to be desired.

Others will put you to the test early. They may ask you questions to see if you know the answers. If you don't, they'll want to see if you'll admit it or if you'll try to bluff your way through it. Some may ask you questions you can't possibly know the answers to yet, for the sheer delight of embarrassing you.

Most—you hope the majority—will adopt a wait-and-see attitude. They're not going to condemn or praise you until they see how you perform. This attitude is healthy and all you really have a right to expect.

You'll be measured initially against your predecessor in the position. If that other's performance was miserable, yours will look great by comparison even if it's mediocre. If you follow a highly capable performer, your adjustment will be tougher. Before you begin thinking it's best to follow a miserable performer, consider the load of tough problems you're inheriting from your inept predecessor; that's why you're there. The highly capable predecessor is probably gone because he or she was promoted. So, in either case, you have a big job ahead of you.

One of your first decisions should be to refrain from immediately instituting changes in the method of operation. (In abnormal situations, top management may have instructed you to go in and make certain immediate changes because of the seriousness of the situation. However, in such cases it is usually announced that changes will be forthcoming.) Above all, be patient. If you make changes immediately, they'll be resented. Your actions will be construed as arrogance and an insult to your predecessor. Many young new leaders make their own life more difficult by assuming they have to use all their new-found power immediately. The keyword should rather be restraint. Whether you want to admit it or not, you're the one who's on trial with your subordinates, not they with you.

This is a good time to make an important point about your own attitude. Many young managers communicate rather well upward to their superiors, but poorly downward to their subordinates. Your subordinates will have more to say about your future than your superiors. You're going to be judged by how well your section or department functions, so the people who now work for you are the most important in your business life. Believe it or not, they're more important even than the president of your company. This bit of knowledge has always seemed obvious to me, yet many new managers spend almost all their time planning their upward communication and give only a passing glance to the people who really control their future.

You undoubtedly know members of the management team who come strolling into the office well after the beginning hour. This is a luxury you can't afford. It's unreasonable to expect subordinates to consider it important to be punctual and start work at the designated time if it's not important to you. Leading by example is still a good concept. This is an area where I recommend that you deviate from your predecessor's practice immediately. Your people will respect you because you observe the same rules that they're expected to observe. The boss who comes in late loses more than the productivity for that hour. That's indeed the smallest part of the lost cost. How do you measure the cost of the halfhearted work that takes place before the top exec comes into the office? It's not that the staff won't work unless they're being watched; rather, they reflect their own manager's attitude. You can't blame them for responding in that manner.

The Personal Touch

Sometime during the first sixty days on the job you should plan on having a personal conversation with each of the people in your area of responsibility. Don't do this the first week or so. Give your subordinates a chance to get used to the idea that you're there. When it comes, the conversation should be formal in nature. Ask your subordinates into your office for an unhurried discussion about anything that's on their mind. Do no more talking yourself than necessary. This first formal discussion is not designed for you to communicate with the others; it's designed to open lines of communication from them to you. (Have you ever noticed that the more you allow the other person to talk, the higher you'll be rated as a brilliant conversationalist?)

Although the employee's personal concerns are important, it's preferable to restrict the discussion to work-related topics. Sometimes it's difficult to define these limits because problems at home may be troubling the employee more than anything else, but at all times you must avoid getting into a situation where you're giving personal advice. Just because you've been anointed as the boss, that doesn't make you an expert on all the personal problems confronting your people. Listen to them; often that's what they need more than anything else—someone to listen to them.

A method I've used in such conversations seems to work rather well. You have to be genuinely interested in people—you can't fake it. The method is to say nothing in the conversation that will tend to terminate it. You must never give the other the sense of being hurried out of the office. For example, the conversation has gone on for only ten minutes and you say, "It sure was great talking to you." The employee will immediately recognize that the statement is meant to terminate the conversation. If your wish to learn what your people are thinking is sincere, you'll avoid what I call *conversation terminators.*

The Conversation Terminator

It may be worthwhile at this point to give further examples of conversation terminators. My purpose is twofold: first, I want you to recognize them when they're used on you; second, I want them to be available for your own use at

13

appropriate times. Although you'll avoid using the device until you're certain the employee you're interviewing has "gotten it all out," it definitely belongs in your management tool chest.

If you've ever had a conversation in someone's office and while you're talking that person reaches over and rests a hand on the telephone receiver even though the telephone hasn't rung, that's a conversation terminator. It says, "As soon as you leave I'm going to make a phone call." Another technique is for the person to pick up a piece of paper from the desk and glance at it periodically during your conversation.

The conversation terminator I particularly like is the one where the host turns in his or her chair behind the desk to a side position as though about to get up. If that doesn't work, the person stands up. That always gets the message across. This approach seems too direct and I personally avoid it, but sometimes it becomes necessary.

It's important that you recognize these conversation terminators. You'll of course try to keep your conversations meaningful enough to preclude their use on you and your use of them on others. There are many more, but you'll compile your own list and find that different people have their own favorite conversation terminators.

Getting to Know Them

Now let's get back to your conversation with your subordinates. The purpose is to give them the opportunity to open communications with you. Show a genuine interest in their concerns; learn what their ambitions are with the company. Ask questions that will get them to expand on their point of view. You can't fake genuine interest in others; you're doing this because you care about the employee's well-being. Such attention is mutually advantageous to both of you. If you can help employees achieve their goals, they'll be more productive, and what's more important they'll feel they're making progress toward their goals.

You'll note that I don't talk about happy employees, because, frankly, I don't know if it's good for a company to have happy employees. Many people think "happy" means satisfied, and a satisfied employee is one who is content. An employee who is content is unlikely to reach out for something better and thus is probably not as productive as he or she could be.

So your goal in these early conversations is to let your subordinates know you care about them as individuals and you're there to help them achieve their goals. Let them know you want to help them solve whatever problems they may be having with the job. Establish a comfort zone in which they can deal with you. Make them feel that it's perfectly natural for them to discuss small problems with you. By discussing small problems and small irritants, most of the larger problems can perhaps be avoided.

You'll discover in your first few months as a manager that your technical abilities are not nearly as important as your human abilities. The majority of your problems are going to revolve around the human and not the technical aspects of the job. Unless your responsibilities are technically complex, you'll find that if you have outstanding human skills you can overlook your minor technical deficiencies. Conversely, even if you're the most technically competent manager in the office, without human skills you'll have great difficulty.

Friends in the Department

One of the problems many new executives confront is their friendship with people in the department who now become their subordinates. This is a difficult situation and I'm sure there's no perfect answer.

It's obvious that you shouldn't have to give up your friendships simply because you've received a promotion. However, you don't want your friendships to hurt your performance or the performance of your friends.

You can't allow your friendships to interfere with your method of operation. A subordinate who's really a friend will understand the dilemma you find yourself in. Precisely this dilemma causes some executives to believe that promoted managers should be brought in from other areas. It minimizes the chances that they'll know their subordinates too well and have close friends within the department.

You must be certain that co-workers who were your friends before you became their supervisor receive the same treatment as everyone else. They must not be treated worse merely to prove to the others how unbiased you are.

If you've usually taken your coffee breaks with certain people in your department, you should consider adopting a rotation policy, so that within a short period you'll have had your coffee break with all your subordinates. This practice seems preferable to discontinuing the sessions and going with fellow supervisors. That would be construed as your moving up the corporate ladder: "His old friends aren't good enough for him any more." If some of the office friends you meet in a social situation include people you now supervise, you must never allow the discussion to deal with the performance of other people in the department.

It's important that everyone you manage be treated with equal fairness. Your friends in the department should be treated the same as everyone else. If you do the right kind of job as supervisor, everyone in the department will consider you a friend.

3

Building confidence

Building confidence is a gradual process. One of your main goals is to develop the confidence of your employees, both in their own abilities and in their opinion of you. They must have confidence that you're competent at your job and that you're fair.

The Success Habit

Building confidence in employees is not an easy task. Do you believe success is habit forming? Failure can also become a habit. Confidence is built on success, so give your people horses they can ride. Especially in dealing with new employees, assign them tasks they can master.Build in them the habit of being successful, starting small with small successes.

Occasionally a subordinate will perform a task incorrectly or just plain blow it. How you handle such situations has a great impact on the confidence of employees. Never correct them in front of others. "Praise in public, criticize in private," the old credo goes—it still has a lot of management truth in it.

Even when you talk to a subordinate in private about an error, your function is to train that person to recognize the nature of the problem so as not to make the same error again. Your attitude about errors will speak louder to an employee than the words you speak. Your statements must be directed toward correcting the misunderstanding that led to the error and not toward personal judgment. Never say or do anything that will make the employee feel inadequate. You want to build confidence, not destroy it. If you get pleasure from making subordinates feel foolish, then you'd better start examining your own motives, because you can't build yourself up by tearing someone else down. Examine the error on the basis of what went wrong, where the misunderstanding occurred, and go on from there. Treat the small error routinely; don't make it bigger than it really is.

You can also build confidence by involving your people in some of the decision-making processes. Without delegating any of your supervisory responsibilites to them, allow them to have some major input into matters that affect them. A new task about to be performed in your area presents the opportunity to give your subordinates some input. Solicit ideas from them on how the new task might best be worked into the daily routine. Given this kind of participation, the new routine will succeed because it's everyone's routine, not just yours. This doesn't mean your staff is making decisions for you; what I'm suggesting is that by involving your people in the process that leads up to your decision, you'll have them working with you rather than accepting new systems imposed on them.

The Evils of Perfectionism

Some managers expect perfection from their employees. They know they won't get it, but they feel they'll get closer to it by demanding it. Unfortunately the executive really believes it. By insisting on perfection you may in fact defeat your own purposes: some employees will become so self-conscious about making a mistake that they slow their performance down to a crawl to make absolutely certain they don't screw up. As a result, production goes way down. The company might be better off with a production of 100 with five errors than with a production of 20 with one error.

Another detriment to being a perfectionist is that everyone resents you for it. Your subordinates believe you're impossible to please and you prove it to them every day. You know what the acceptable standards for work performance are in your company; no one can blame you for wanting to be better than the average; but you'll have far more success if you get the employees involved in helping decide how to improve performance. If it's their plan, you have a significantly better chance of achieving your goal.

You can also build confidence by developing esprit de corps within your own area. Make sure, however, that the feeling you build is supportive of the prevailing company spirit and not in competition with it.

The Limitations of Power

During the thirties, when there was a lot of unemployment, companies demanded respect for executives and employees adhered to company methods and procedures without question. I suppose there are still some managers around today who'd love to be able to issue orders and have their every wish carried out as though they were back in "the good old days." It takes a more highly qualified person to be a leader in the business world today, where your instructions are questioned and you spend some time persuading and not a great deal of time issuing dictatorial orders. Only rarely should the enlightened manager have to reach back and use naked power to get things done.

There are some who believe that if you have the power, you use it. The enlightened manager seldom uses power, not from fear of using it, but because its use is unnecessary. You don't have to go around with a sign on your lapel that says "Boss." Everyone knows you're in charge; issuing orders unnecessarily merely adds an aggressive element: "I'm boss and you better believe it!" Managers who are most successful in dealing with others seldom reach back and use the authority they have. They're able to get the job done without "pulling rank." If the only way you can get routine jobs done is to use all the authority you have, what are you going to do when you have a serious problem?

Attitudes are discussed at length in a subsequent chapter. Your own attitude is important in building confidence. Your subordinates can sense more about your attitude than you suspect. They learn to understand your moods and they find out where your triggering mechanisms are. Therefore, work to be consistent in your behavior so that your employees aren't continually surprised by your fluctuating attitudes and actions.

You'll find that your concern for and efforts toward building your employees' confidence will do a great deal in fortifying your own self-confidence. It's similar to the old cliché about the teacher gaining the most from a learning experience. However, this isn't the only way to build your own confidence.

You also build it by making correct decisions. Each time you score well with a solid decision, confidence in your ability to make judgments is reinforced.

Decision Making

This naturally leads to the subject of decision making. Some people agonize over every decision they have to make.

If making decisions is a constant irritation for you, you should seriously consider getting out of management. Life is too short to be spent in a state of turmoil every day. There are surely plenty of jobs that are challenging and financially rewarding and that require talent but not the talent to make decisions.

I see two basic reasons why some people have trouble making decisions. First, they're not sure they have all the information necessary to make a decision; second, they're afraid of making a mistake and having to suffer its consequences.

It's unlikely that you'll ever be able to gather 100 percent of the information that might apply to a given business situation. Even if you think you have all there is, you could find a new bit of information a few days later that proves otherwise. If you've been reasonable and prudent in gathering the information you need, even though by spending more time you might get that last 5 percent, go ahead and make the decision. It's highly unlikely that having that additional 5 percent would have led you to a different judgment.

It goes without saying that you'll blow one once in a while. All you're after is to be correct most of the time. I won't use the cliché about the baseball player who bats .300 —in business you can't afford to make correct judgments only three times out of ten. That would mean being wrong seven times out of ten. As you get more experience you'll find that you're making correct decisions 99 percent of the time, because in most situations the answer is obvious and you're being asked to reinforce someone else's judgment. Many problems are brought to you because a subordinate wants your agreement and approval before proceeding. Entire books have been written about the decision-making process. Common sense will provide the correct answer in most managerial situations. If you remember nothing else that's been said so far about the decision-making process, remember this: You can get into more management difficulty by repeatedly refusing to make decisions than by occasionally making an incorrect one.

4

The "we and they" syndrome

"I don't know why *they* made that rule."
"They certainly don't understand the people on the firing line."
"If *they* only knew how *we* feel about such practices."
"I don't know what *we* can do about it when *they* issue such dumb regulations."

You can come up with many more examples. The "we and they" syndrome indicates a state of mind that regards *they* as the enemy. Who *they* are depends on who *you* are. *They* can include all those who are one level or more above you, or it can be restricted to the top management of the company. *We* is you and anyone you consider a peer.

Now that you're a manager you might as well accept the fact that you're part of the *they* you and your peer group used to talk about when you were still a member in good standing of the *we*. You're not going to be able to make the *we* and *they* disappear because of your promotion. To some members of the *we* you're a traitor because you crossed over and became a member of the *they*.

The largest restraint placed on members of the *we* group is the limitation that exists in their own minds. Recognition of the we and they syndrome is important. It puts the action of many people in its proper perspective.

Many recently promoted managers fall prey to the feeling that they're still in a *we* group, but that the *we* is now their own management group. In other words, it's a switch of labels. Don't fall into this trap. Rise above this kind of thinking. From now on, there should be only the single *we* group that includes everyone in the organization.

You won't change everyone. You may not change anyone but yourself. But you're the most important person under your control and that's a solid beginning. You can at least put your own thinking in its proper perspective. Perhaps we have hold of a great truth here. Maybe the problems of this planet could be reduced if more of its inhabitants would start thinking in terms of *we* instead of *they*.

The thought may enter your mind that the author is suggesting aspects of an attitude that go beyond the question of management. That may be true. But your job is so large a part of your life, and it spills over into so many other aspects of your daily activities, that the point is worth making.

5

Looking above and below

We all know people who relate and communicate very well upward and maybe even sideward in an organization, but very poorly downward to their subordinates. (Upward, sideward, and downward are of course references to standings on the organization chart.)

If I get only one idea across to you in this chapter, the effort will be worth it. The thought is that your subordinates have more control over your future than your superiors. This seems perfectly obvious, but it's amazing how many managers ignore it. They'll write great memos to their boss but do a rotten job of communicating with their own people.

Your promotability will be determined, not on the basis of how well you may fit into the new job or what your prospects of success in it are, but on how well you perform it. Even if you're satisfied with your current position, you'll be more content performing it well than performing it poorly.

Genuine Concern

One way to perform your job well is to give full attention to the needs of the people in your area of responsibility. Some leaders make the mistake of thinking that the concern they show for their subordinates will be interpreted as a sign of weakness. Genuine concern, indeed, is a sure sign of strength. Showing interest in the welfare of your people doesn't mean you'll "cave in" to unreasonable demands. Unfortunately, many new executives fail to recognize this. They're unable to differentiate between concern and weakness.

Your concern must of course be genuine. You can't fake it. By genuine concern I mean seeing that your people are properly challenged, and that they're appropriately rewarded when they perform well.

You can't start off by complacently telling yourself "I'm going to be Mr. Nice Guy." You must seriously take on the burden of responsibility for these people. In fact, all of you are mutually responsible to one another. Your subordinates now look to you for leadership. You must see to it that the objectives of the company and the objectives of your subordinates are not at cross-purposes. Your people should realize that they can achieve their own objectives only by doing their part in helping the company achieve its overall goals.

The person they look to for leadership is you. You serve as interpreter for the employee. What is the company's policy? You'd better be certain that you know what it is!

Showing Fairness

Another of your responsibilities is to make sure that work in your area is fairly and properly distributed so that no one is being carried along by the others or is doing more than a reasonable share of the carrying. In many offices, work assignments will vary; in others, nearly everyone will perform the same function. The supervisory task in the latter situation is much easier as far as equality of workload is concerned. It has other problems, however, in that relationships among the employees are likely to be more strained. Too many of the people will then spend their time worrying about distribution of work down to a gnat's eyelid. You don't have to be that exact. Your approach should be equitable without being scientifically equal.

I think it's more interesting to manage a section (unit, division, department) where a wide variety of tasks are performed. You'll receive a variety of questions ranging from the routine clerical to the more complex professional inquiry. The questions are important to the questioner so you give attention to all of them. You've probably seen the card in many executive offices: "Go ahead and ask your dumb question. It's easier to handle than a dumb mistake."

Variety Among Your Subordinates

You'll find people in your area who aren't interested in promotion. One reason is that they don't want to be responsible for the actions of others. Such persons, however, might be interested in being promoted if the new position doesn't require supervising other people. There are many employees who want to be responsible only for themselves, and their kind of personality is also needed in business and industry. We'd have a rather chaotic business environment if everyone was highly oriented toward managing everyone else.

In dealing with people who prefer not to work closely with anyone else, by all means put them in situations where their performance depends only on themselves. Some peo-

27

ple are loners all the way. Then there are the *work loners,* who want to be left alone when it comes to the job but who are not necessarily antisocial. They'll go for coffee with their co-workers, have lunch with them, and even see them socially away from the office. Many workers respond best to the team approach. They need to feel they're part of a unit and they'll develop great loyalty to their team. They'll perform well if you can put them into a team situation.

It's obvious that you can't get everyone into the ideal situation, but knowing that different people have different approaches to their work will make you a more effective manager. In other words, get people into situations where they're comfortable and you'll get a better performance from them.

Dealing with Your Superiors

We've spent some time talking about your attitude toward your subordinates; it's only proper that we pay attention also to your attitude toward your superiors. Your future success indeed depends more on your subordinates than on your superiors, but it would be disastrous to ignore those who outrank you.

If you've just had a big promotion, you're feeling grateful to your boss. You're also pleased that the top exec was perceptive enough to have recognized the talent you have. But your new responsibility demands a new level of loyalty from you. After all, you're now a part of the management team. You can't be a good team member without identifying with the team.

Remember, however, that being your superior in the company doesn't necessarily make that person smarter than you. Your boss may be more experienced than you, may have been with the company longer, may have come from the right family, or may be in the top position for other reasons. But it's also possible that your boss performed exceedingly well and is indeed smarter than you.

Loyalty to Them

Being loyal has fallen into widespread disrepute. Blind loyalty has never had much to recommend it, but being loyal doesn't mean selling your soul to the devil. Your company and your boss are not out to rip off the world. If they are, they're not worth being loyal to. More important, you shouldn't be working for them.

So let's assume you're convinced that your company's purpose is commendable and you're pleased to be associated with its goals. The kind of loyalty we're talking about has to do with carrying out policies or decisions you morally support. Your position with your company, let's again assume, allows you some input into decisions having to do with your own area of responsibility. In making such input, you must see that it's as thoughtful and as broadly based as possible. Don't be the kind of narrow-sighted executive whose recommendations are designed to benefit only one's own area of responsibility. When this happens, it won't be long before the advice isn't sought because what's offered is too parochial.

If you make recommendations that are broadly based and represent the greater good of the company, your advice will be sought more often. This doesn't mean you're continually offering up your own people as sacrificial lambs. Keep everything in balance.

The important thing is your involvement in the decision-making process beyond your own managerial level. Occasionally a decision or policy will be made that's directly contrary to the opinions you've expressed; you'll be expected to support that decision or policy and you may even have to implement it.

Ask your boss why the decision was made, if you don't already know. Find out what important considerations went into formulation of the policy. Determine what you can about the processes that led to the decision. The old idea that you follow blindly no longer holds much water. That kind of loyalty happened a lot during the Great Depression when jobs were scarce and everyone who held a job wanted desperately to keep it. We should be grateful that this approach no longer applies. Nonetheless, many managers and supervisors doubtless wish it were still true, because today's more democratic approach requires people to be better managers. No longer can you bark orders and expect others to wag their tail and roll over like your favorite puppy.

If you're to do an outstanding job of supervision, you have a right to understand the reasons behind major company decisions and company policy. Perhaps your own manager is one who follows higher authority blindly and guards information about top management as if all of it were top secret—and you're the enemy. In that case you may have to be a lot more political in how you go about getting the answers to your question.

If it's a policy that affects other departments, you can find out from people at your own organizational level in those departments. If a friend in Department X has a boss who shares information freely with subordinates, it may be relatively simple to find out what you want to know over a cup of coffee with your friend.

Their Fallibility

In dealing with superiors, it's important to recognize that in addition to their strengths they have weaknesses; you'll have to learn to work with and around those weaknesses. Someone once said that the way to get ahead is to make your boss look good. I think that's true, so long as it doesn't put

30

you at cross-purposes with the company's objectives. Loyalty to the organization and loyalty to your superior should never be allowed to become a conflict of interests. If by being loyal to your superior you have to be disloyal to the organization, then it's simply something you cannot do. Of course, making your boss look good may fit into your overall method for dealing with your superior. But if that strategy results in your boss's unwillingness ever to let you go, that could stand in the way of promotional opportunities. I'll talk more about preparing yourself for a promotion in a later chapter.

The honeymoon is over

6

Changing the employee

Psychologists are fond of saying that the only way to change people is through a traumatic experience, a religious conversion, or brain surgery. I don't know whether the assertion is completely true, but it does point to the difficulty we encounter when we try to make basic changes in someone's personality. It's like the woman who marries the alcoholic because she feels it's her mission in life to change him. She may indeed change him if she's a traumatic experience for him.

But people don't really change their basic personality. Taking slovenly workers and trying to make them meticulous and neat is probably going to be an impossible task. You can smoothe out "minor bumps" in their personalities and cause them to modify their behavior on the job, but you aren't going to create a permanent personality change.

Accommodation

We should rather attempt to put people into situations where they already have the natural traits essential for performing the task well. If a particular job requires a perfectionist, you certainly don't fill the position with a person who hates details and then experiment with behavior modification to get a satisfactory performance. You're much better off assigning the job to someone who not only has demonstrated skill with details but who enjoys such work. I'll talk more about this in the chapter on hiring employees.

There are ways to accommodate an employee that are simple and effective. Transfer the employee to a job that's more in keeping with his or her capacities. Too often people are moved through an organization in a rigid line of succession. And too often managers don't consider that they may be removing subordinates from their comfort zone. Usually, jobs become broader in nature as they become more important. People who like detail, who cross every "t" and dot every "i," are usually uncomfortable when they move away from such detail. Thank God for people who like such trivia, who'll clean up after some of us "Big Picture" hotshots. To paraphrase a psychologist I know, "Show me a person with a lot of drive and I'll show you a nit-picking perfectionist following behind and cleaning up the mess."

Both types of personalities are needed in an organization. Don't expect your employees to handle all aspects of their job perfectly. They'll do better with elements of the job they like than with those they dislike. I've always tried to follow the rule in the office that I'll do those things first that I dislike so that I can get them out of the way and spend the rest of the day doing the things I like.

Has it ever occurred to you that most of the problems in a working environment are related to the attitude of people toward the work and toward each other? We spend endless time trying to change our co-workers to conform to our idea of what they ought to be. This is a complete waste of effort. We ought to attempt instead to put people in jobs where they can develop their natural traits and their natural preferences. Just because we're interested in promotion, we assume everyone else is. In our grandiose "Horatio Alger" business environment, we assume everyone wants to move up the ladder and become the boss.

That is not true. Many people merely want to do their job; they want to be responsible for no one besides themselves and they want to be able to forget the workplace when they walk out of it at night. They get their reward and their challenge from other things. Most people rate family ahead of job, health ahead of job, spiritual well-being ahead of job; many rate hobbies and recreational interest ahead of their job. They perform satisfactorily on the job, but turn you off when you talk about more responsibility and golden opportunity to move up the ladder.

Natural Followers

We meet people who say they want to be promoted, because getting ahead has been so drilled into the American subconscious that to admit you don't want to get ahead almost makes you un-American. So people mouth the words and nod their heads at the appropriate moments, but in their secret hearts they don't want to be promoted. They don't want to accept more responsibility. They tip you off in many ways—you have to be perceptive enough to pick up the clues. They'll avoid any task that requires joint work. If they do take on joint work, they'll do most of it themselves because only then can they be sure it's done correctly. Or they'll wash their hands of the entire matter and let the other person do 90 percent of the work.

In group meetings such people will seldom offer ideas. When pumped for their thoughts, they'll say little that will commit them to anything of substance. They don't stick out their neck. They realize that sticking out your neck means running the risk that someone may try to chop it off. That hurts, and these people don't want to be hurt. They're the

37

salt of the earth, and American industry would be dead without them. If everyone wanted to be promoted into the executive ranks, the competition would be so tough that you and I would perhaps never make it. We should thank our lucky stars every night that not everyone wants our job. To be effective, a leader must have people to lead, and the people I've been describing make great followers.

A Last Resort: Dismissal or Transfer

Another way to accommodate employees is to replace them. This could amount to an outright dismissal or a transfer to another area of the company. It's a procedure we should spend some time developing. Too often, in large offices, managers unload their problem employees onto another department through the promotion route. When asked by the manager of that other department how the prospective promotee is performing in the current job, they're not completely candid in their reply. I think the only correct policy in this situation is to be completely candid, because you'll someday yourself be looking at people in other departments as candidates for promotion into your own department. Your best guarantee of not getting someone else's rejects is never to deliver that kind of cheap shot yourself.

I actually had that happen to me once. In going to the personnel department and looking at the performance appraisals of people one level below the job we were attempting to fill in our division, we ended up with three likely candidates. As is customary, I called the supervisors of these candidates and got a glowing report about one in particular, a man. We promoted him to our department and he ended up being a complete disaster. We had to terminate him after a short period of time because he wasn't doing the job. I then confronted the person who had made the recommendation and asked for an explanation, never dreaming I had been mousetrapped. The answer I got was that the employee had not been satisfactory but might become so if given another opportunity. By not being candid, they tricked me into doing their dirty work for them.

There's of course a great temptation to pay back such a department in kind, but the solution is to make sure no one ever does that to you in the first place. Retaliation in an intercompany operation is not beneficial to anyone.

Rehabilitation

There'd be nothing wrong, however, in attempting to rehabilitate a nonproductive employee if it were done with the full knowledge of everyone involved. In the situation where I was victimized, for example, had my fellow manager sat down with me and indicated that the employee was not doing a good job *but* there were strong reasons for wanting him to have another chance, I might have taken the man. I've known of such trials that have been successful. The work and the worker were not a good fit, but the worker had talent; the move to another area where that talent could be used turned a less-than-satisfactory employee into a productive one. Generally, however, you'll be more effective as a leader if you can solve your own problems in your own department and not unload them onto another department. Companies use many testing devices to put people on jobs that come naturally to them, or at least in working areas of some personal preference. These devices range all the way from simple five-minute tests to complex three-hour psychological evaluations. This is something your company either already has or should consider having. To emphasize my point again, you must always be conscious of the advantages of fitting employees to jobs at which they have the best chance of being successful. It's much easier to move people around into jobs that are natural for them than to force them into jobs they perform poorly and then try to "educate" them. It just doesn't work. Some psychologists think major changes in our personalities are unlikely to occur after age 16.

Individual Style: Benefits and Detriments

Whenever possible, allow your subordinates to individualize the job as much as they can while still maintaining the quality, quantity, and objectives that have to be maintained to achieve company goals. The more you can allow your people to bring their own personality into the job, the better the chance of their being successful at it. The higher the position on the organization chart, the greater the latitude usually allowed for individual styling of that position.

Although it's important that you allow your subordinates to mold the job to their own personality, you have to keep them from riding their own occupational hobbyhorses. Some people will put an overwhelming emphasis on things they like to do, but these may not represent your own priorities in that particular situation. In every job, certain tasks are more important than others. As long as you and the employee agree about the relative importance of certain tasks and attend to them in that order of priority, you won't have a problem. You will have a problem where tasks you consider important are considered unimportant by the employee. You're then working in the reverse order of importance called for by the job. Too often we do the things we like to do first and continually put off doing disagreeable tasks. But in business the supervisor's order of priority always takes precedence over an employee's. A later chapter, "Organizing Your Own Time"—may be helpful in clarifying these matters.

Priorities

One of the biggest errors executives make is in not letting their employees know what work is considered the most important from the company's point of view. They take the attitude that it's all important. That puts employees in the position of deciding what should be done at what time. You can't then blame your subordinates if their sense of priorities ends up different from your own. You must discuss the situation with each employee, and of course the best time to have such a discussion is when the employee first moves into the job.

Subtle shifts repeatedly occur defining the workload and its importance; to stay on top of your sense of priorities you have to make sure you and your subordinates are constantly on the same wavelength.

It has often been said that people resist change. That's generally true, but a more precise statement is that people resist change when it's introduced too rapidly. If you can introduce change gradually your people will accept it. In completely changing the rules so that it appears there's been a radical redefinition of the job, you're asking for real trouble unless the employees understand the reason for the change. They're being told to move out of their comfort zone; every habit they've formed and every bit of training they've received is being completely ignored. This is why introducing change gradually is much more acceptable. Most operational changes can be introduced on a gradual basis. In the few cases where they have to be introduced radically, perhaps overnight, you have no choice. You must then absolutely and thoroughly explain the necessity for the change.

Managing Change

All of us make changes in our work habits and in our personality, but they're so gradual that we never recognize them as change. Take a woman who worked on a particular job ten years ago; bring her back to the workplace today; she'll be amazed by the changes that have occurred in the job. A fellow worker who has remained on the job throughout those years, however, will be virtually unaware of the changes—*if* they were all introduced on a gradual basis. The more accurate statement, therefore, is that people resist uncomfortable change. Make the change comfortable for them by introducing it in small increments, and they won't fight you as severely.

What people say about change and the attitudes they display toward it are often quite different. A lot of people say, "I just love variety," but watch them on the job and it's obvious that they're most content when working in what can be described as their "comfort zone." The reason for this contradiction is that it's socially acceptable to want variety in your job, whereas it's not socially acceptable to be rigid or inflexible. Thus, even people who are rigid and inflexible will seldom admit it. It's not unlike the human relations situation. That is, we're a society so oriented toward having good human relations that we all claim to like working with people. A lot of us in fact prefer to work alone, but it's not socially acceptable to say we don't like to work with people and so we don't say it.

7

Disciplining the employee

There are obviously performance standards your area of responsibility must meet. These may vary by different companies, by the nature of the work, and even by departments. They may also vary within a department. The important point as it affects discipline is that all employees must know what standards they're expected to comply with. You create nasty problems for yourself in trying to discipline an employee on the basis of nebulous work standards.

Let's assume you've done a satisfactory job of establishing standards for each job. In all probability those standards are written into a job description. The job description indicates the elements of accountability that apply to the job; you can therefore measure the individual against those standards. Now you must have methods within your area of responsibility that allow you to be constantly aware of how people are performing in relationship to the standards. You can't operate on the assumption that unless you're hearing complaints from customers, or other departments, the performance is acceptable. If you wait for warning signals in that manner, severe damage may already have been done.

Prior Knowledge

Your own attitude about performance is crucial. The place and time for conveying your attitude about performance to employees is when they first step into the job. They need to know exactly what's expected of them. Performance standards will change. During the training period you'll accept less in the way of quality and quantity than afterward. You should have this properly backstopped during the training period so that their errors don't get beyond your own department.

Feedback is critical to proper and effective discipline. You must know as soon as possible when performance is substandard so that it can be corrected immediately. Let's assume, however, that you've set adequate standards. Also, the employee knows what those standards are. Further, you have an adequate method of feedback so that you know when substandard performance is a problem.

The Private Conference

One of the oldest rules about disciplining an employee is that it should always be done in private. Never humiliate an employee, even in cases of dismissal. (Dismissal is covered in another chapter.) The employee must always be made to understand that the performance is being criticized, not the person. This is one of the most difficult attitudes for a manger to convey. Many people are unable to differentiate between criticism of their work and criticism of themselves. They consider criticism of their work a personal affront. You have to work very hard at making sure they understand it has nothing to do with whether or not you like them. You must convey the idea that you both have a mutual interest in bringing the substandard performance up to a satisfactory level.

Religiously avoid making statements that can be interpreted as a personal attack. Never say, "I want to talk to you about your mistake." Never say, "You made a mistake." Never say, "You're not performing well." Such statements will only result in your having to spend most of your time trying to get the employee into a positive frame of mind so you can discuss the performance of the work. Rather, approach the problem on the assumption that the employee wants to do a good job. The vast majority of the time that will be true. People want to perform well. They have nothing to gain by performing badly, unless they want to be fired.

Attack the substandard performance by viewing it as the result of some misunderstanding about how the work should be done. Perhaps the employee has missed something in the training process, and this has created a systems deficiency that's causing the work to fall below the company's standards. By taking this approach, you inform the employee from the outset that you're talking about the performance and not the person.

Give and Take

You should not want the conversation to be a monologue. Many managers do all of the talking, meanwhile building up resentment in the party on the receiving end. You need to encourage the employee's participation in the conversation. Without it there's a good chance you won't solve the problem.

Be careful, now, and don't go overboard! Some executives, in their effort to be scrupulously fair, become so cautious and tactful that the employee leaves their office expecting to get a raise for outstanding performance. You have to make certain that your subordinate understands that the work is not up to standards. How you say it, though, is critically important.

When bringing the employee into your office, put him or her at ease. This may not seem like a big thing to you, but to an employee who doesn't often enter the sanctum of the high and mighty, you're the boss and being called into your presence may be a frightening prospect. Therefore, do everything you can to make the other comfortable.

Encourage the employee to participate in the discussion early in the game. You might start off with a statement like this: "Fred, you've been with us three months now and I think it's time we had a conversation about how you're getting along. As you know, I have a great interest in your being successful on this job. How do you feel things are going?"

By using this approach, you encourage an employee who is not performing up to standards to bring up the subject. It seldom comes as a surprise to an employee to learn that specified standards are not being met. Surprise is likely only if the employee has never been told what is expected. If that's the case, you really have some serious problems—problems of training and communication.

As the employee describes how things are going, you direct the conversation to the standards that are not being met. For example, you ask, "Do you think you're getting close to the standards we've established for experienced employees?" If the answer is yes, you could ask, "Do you believe you're performing at the same level as an experienced employee?" If the answer is again yes, then the employee may be out of touch with reality. The point is to continue asking questions of this type until you get the kind of response that will lead you into discussion of the quality of the work.

Obviously, if all your tactful efforts have failed to induce the employee to bring up the crucial subject, then you have no choice but to insert it into the conversation yourself. To the employee who persists in asserting that things are going well, you could say, "That's an interesting observation you've made about the quality of the work, because my observation indicates that it's not up to the standards we've set for the job. Why do you suppose my information is different from yours?" You then have the matter out on the desk for discussion.

Eliminate Misunderstanding

As you proceed further into the conversation, you use techniques that ensure that the employee knows what's expected. It's a good idea to get feedback on what you've mutually agreed upon, so that there can be no misunderstanding later about what was said.

One way to make certain of this is to write a memorandum at the conclusion of the conversation and place it in the employee's file. This becomes particularly important if you're managing a lot of people and it's possible that six months from now you won't remember the details of the conversation.

The Primacy of the Person

There are problems about an employee's performance that cannot be separated from the person. When talking about the quality or quantity of an employee's work, it's obvious that the techniques I've just discussed can help in establishing firmly in the employee's mind that a difference exists between your criticism of the work and your view of the person. But with certain attitudinal problems it's more difficult to make the distinction, and in many cases it can't be done.

Let's assume you have a highly satisfactory employee who can't seem to get to work on time. Disciplining unsatisfactory employees is easier than handling a discipline problem with one like this who you obviously want to keep for the company. But what happens in such situations is that no matter how superior the performance, if you allow the employee the privilege of coming in late every day, you're going to create a morale problem with the rest of the people who adhere to the office hours. (What I'm saying obviously does not apply if your office has gone to flexible working hours.)

In talking with the satisfactory employee about this problem, one of the better approaches is to explain the management difficulties you'd have if every employee ignored the working hours. You couldn't tolerate that situation. In addition, the employee is creating difficulties for himself or herself. You can then go into the discussion in some detail and start working on a solution. Let's follow through with this problem of the tardy employee, because it happens often enough that you'll eventually have to face it.

Most conscientious employees who are doing a satisfactory job will react positively to your statements. You may notice that for the next ten days or so they appear at their desk on time. At that point you'll be feeling pretty smug about your success in managing people. You'll find, however, that when the pressure is off, the reformed employees will be coming in late again. You can't take a casual approach about this and assume it was just an unusual set of circumstances. All your subordinates must be made to know you expect them to be on time every day.

I would recommend that the first time this happens after your initial conversation, you again have a discussion with the offender. This doesn't have to be a full-blown dialogue of the same length and detail as the first one. All you need to do is reinforce what you said previously. There may have been a sound reason for the latest tardiness, and it could be that the second conversation will keep the employee on the straight and narrow. If you can get to the point where the employee is coming to work on time for approximately six months, you may assume you've changed that person's work patterns enough so that you no longer have a serious problem. What you should expect from that point on is the same attendance as you get from the rest of your employees.

Some Personal Experiences

I had something of this kind happen to me a number of years ago. The only difference from the situation just described is that this employee's performance was only slightly better than mediocre. I couldn't in clear conscience say the man was a satisfactory employee. He was barely good enough to avoid being fired for incompetence. It got so bad that the people who worked around him nicknamed him "Sleepy." He really didn't come alive until about 10:00 A.M. I thought his first two tardinesses might have just cause, but became concerned when the new employee didn't volunteer a reason for being late. So on the third tardiness I had a talk with him and was told that he had difficulty getting started in the mornings. I sympathized with him; I had the same problem. I then suggested a game: since the man was repeatedly arriving ten minutes late, he should set the clocks in his house forward fifteen minutes. He said he'd try this, but he found that it didn't work. I then decided on a different approach.

I asked the employee if there was any physical reason for his having trouble getting started in the morning, perhaps anemia. He said that was not the case; he just was unable to get going in the morning. He had had this trouble all his life, through school and on his previous job.

The previous job had been in a small office where being on time was not considered critical. I then explained why it was important in the current situation, since the company employed a great number of people. In allowing one person to have a different starting time from all the rest, we created a problem as far as equitable treatment of employees was concerned. I then suggested the possibility of his going to bed earlier at night, and discovered the man was already sleeping twelve hours a night. I again told him it was very important that he solve the problem; in fact, his job depended on it.

I must admit that the situation did get better for about a week, but then the employee started slipping back into the old tardiness routine again. I need hardly add that the man had no trouble leaving on time at the end of the day. Following several further conversations with the offender, I ended by terminating him.

The situation just described is one that many executives would view as a failure of management skills. That's wrong. Not every personnel problem can be solved by accommodation. As far as I was concerned, I had done everything I could to remedy the situation, even to the point of suggesting that the employee visit his doctor for help. Since nothing I did worked, the only solution I had was to change to a new employee.

It's possible that you'll have other problems of a similar nature, such as too much time spent on coffee breaks, overstaying the lunch hour, or situations that involve being at the desk at a certain time. Needless to say, you don't run a sweat shop, and everyone will occasionally be tardy at some time or other. What's critical is dealing effectively with chronic offenders who create management problems for you and the organization.

Another difficult problem that you wouldn't expect in this day and age is cleanliness. This did happen to me once— and unexpectedly, having to do with a woman. The people working around her complained about the aroma emanating from her area. I avoided facing up to the problem because I was a new, young supervisor at the time and wasn't sure how to handle it. Eventually, I did face it and did have a conversation with the woman. She assured me that she bathed daily; we finally arrived at the joint conclusion that perhaps she wasn't getting her clothing dry-cleaned or washed as often as necessary to solve the problem. She did solve the problem, but left three months later, I think out of personal embarrassment.

If I had that one to handle over again, I believe I'd arrange to have someone in personnel talk directly to the employee rather than do it myself. The reason would not be to avoid a difficult situation, but rather to spare the woman embarrassment every time she saw me and the misery of being constantly reminded of the uncomfortable conversation. By having someone in personnel talk to her away from her work area, the problem might have been solved and I might have been able to salvage an otherwise satisfactory employee. As it turned out, the woman moved out of town shortly after she quit, because her husband was transferred by his employer to another location, so I'd have lost her anyway.

Another situation that I recall along this line involved a man who was handling punch cards that were passed along from one area to another. I received a complaint because the man was always picking his ears and the person receiving the work from him didn't like handling soiled cards. I felt that the complaint might be legitimate, however I decided against discussing it with the offender. Rather, I suggested to the man doing the complaining that he was perhaps being a little overly critical. I didn't say it in exactly that manner, but I let the man know that I didn't consider it quite as serious as he did. It was one of those problems that went away by itself.

This might be the place to make the observation that sometimes doing nothing is the right approach to solving a problem. But you have to be careful not to adopt a laissez-faire method of management and assume that many problems will solve themselves.

The Disciplinary Approach

Getting to matters of greater seriousness, you might use a disciplinary approach in situations where you're attempting to correct performance. For example, you have a highly satisfactory employee whose work sharply deteriorates. Needless to say, you're continually communicating with the employee about the deterioration. You want to retain the employee, but you find that your words are not being taken seriously. In a situation like that you may recommend zero salary increase for the employee for that year, with a full explanation as to why you're doing it. Inform the employee in advance that if the work doesn't get better there'll be no increase in pay. Having made that threat or stated that possibility of action, you must then follow through on it so that you don't lose credibility. Some people don't actually believe you'll take such action. It's a technique that frequently works because people still care about the paycheck.

Another disciplinary technique you can use is to put the employee on probation. Say you have work deterioration that needs to be corrected and you want to give the employee every opportunity to correct it. You must make it perfectly clear that the substandard level of work being delivered cannot be allowed to continue. Also, you should set a deadline for a resolution to the problem. You might say to the employee, "This problem has to be solved within one month or we'll have to make other arrangements."

But first the employee must be made to understand exactly what kind of performance is being labeled substandard. The employee must also know how to correct it, and must know what level of performance is expected. You musn't arrive at the end of the probationary period only to find a legitimate difference of opinion as to how the employee is performing. The standards must be set so clearly that no disagreement about whether they've been met or not is possible. They must be measurable standards. You must keep a satisfactory set of records, because you may have to justify firing the employee if it comes to that.

Records are also helpful in raising performance standards. You can use the records to show your subordinates how they improved the quality of their work. This becomes an added gain because the employees are inspired to greater effort by pride in their accomplishment.

New employees in a company are often put on probation, either in line with standard company policy or as individual cases. You can't establish a probationary period for every employee in your department or division if it's not a companywide practice. Many companies use a 90-day probationary period. Employees doing satisfactory work at the end of that time are taken off the probationary rolls and become regular employees. It's also customary to give a modest salary increase in recognition of satisfactory completion of the probationary course. If the work is not satisfactory at that point, the employee should anticipate being terminated. Again, it should never come as a surprise.

The Mood Modifier

Some executives use a technique that I refer to as the *mood modifier.* This is pretty subtle, and it takes a good actor to pull it off. I'm not sure I recommend it, but you should be aware of it in case it's ever pulled on you. As the name of the technique implies, the manager modifies the mood of the conversation in dealing with an employee whose performance is not satisfactory. This is done to avoid direct examination of the issue. Letting an employee know you're dissatisfied by appearing to be irritated is unfair, however, because the employee may misinterpret what it is that's troubling you. The imagined inadequacy may not be the one you had in mind at all.

All of us, from time to time at the office, fall under the spell of moods that reflect outside situations that are troubling us. Many books on management tell us we must leave our problems at the door, or at home, and not bring them into the office. I think that attitude is naive, because few people can completely shut off a personal problem and keep it from affecting how they perform on the job.

There's no doubt, however, that you can minimize the impact a problem has on your work. The first step is to admit that something is irritating you and that it may affect your relationship with your co-workers. If you can do that, you probably won't end by making the others victims of whatever your personal problem is. If an outside problem is gnawing at you and you have to deal with an employee in a critical situation, I see nothing wrong with saying to the employee, "Look, I'm really not in the greatest mood today. If I seem a little irritated, I hope you'll forgive me." This kind of candor is refreshing to a subordinate.

Never think for a moment that the others don't have the ability to judge your moods. By showing dramatic changes of mood, you become less effective. In addition, your subordinates will know when to expect these changes, what the telltale signs are, and they'll avoid dealing with you when you're on the bottom swing of such a mood. They'll wait until you're on the high end of the pendulum.

Managing Your Feelings

You should work hard at being even-tempered. But I don't think it's a good idea to be the kind of manager who's bothered by nothing. I'm talking about the person who never seems to feel great joy, great sorrow, great anything. People will not identify with you if they believe you disguise all your feelings.

Keeping your cool all the time is another matter. There are good reasons for keeping your cool. If you can always remain fairly calm, even in troubled situations, you're more likely to think clearly and so be in a better position to handle tough problems. But it's also important that you show feelings once in a while, or people will think you're a management robot.

To be an outstanding manager of people, you have to care about people. That doesn't mean taking a missionary or social-worker approach toward them, but if you enjoy their company and respect their feelings, you'll be much more effective in your job than the supervisor who's mostly "thing" oriented.

This, indeed, is one of the problems companies bring on themselves when they assume that the most efficient worker in an area is the one who should be promoted to management. That worker may be efficient because of being "thing" oriented. Moving such "experts" into areas where they supervise others doesn't automatically make them "people" oriented.

Hiring and training new employees

There are probably as many different hiring practices as there are companies. If I were to attempt to cover all the various methods I'd never get to the end of this chapter, so let's make a couple of simple assumptions. Let's say the personnel department does the initial screening, but you have the ultimate decision-making authority as to who comes to work in your area of responsibility.

The Use of Tests

With greater federal, state, and sometimes city participation in hiring procedures, your company may not do much testing of prospective employees. I'm aware of one company that has done away with all tests. It uses a method that I call *post-hiring tests.* These make it possible to fire people early in the game if they don't cut the mustard.

This is the most expensive method of testing I can think of. I suspect it's an overreaction to government involvement in hiring procedures. Companies may increasingly resort to this method as their frustration levels increase. In so doing they make the problems of management more difficult, not to mention the psychological damage done to people who are fired when their only mistake was in having been hired in the first place.

The quality of prospective employees will vary a great deal. When unemployment rates are high, you'll find greater interest being shown in the job and you'll have a larger number of prospects to choose from. The reverse will be true when unemployment rates are low. I've known situations where available employees were so few that you'd consider hiring anyone who appeared at your desk. So there'll be forces out of your control. We're concerned here with situations you can control.

If tests are used by your personnel department, consider first those that are relevant to the position to be filled. Math aptitude may not be important if you're hiring for a typing or secretarial job; ability to spell would be more to the point.

The Screening Process

The way to begin your screening is by thoroughly reviewing the job description. Some managers make the mistake of wanting the applicant to do better than average on all the tests. If you take that approach you could very well pass up a person who would do an outstanding job for you.

Your interview with the prospect is a two-way "sizing-up" meeting. Naturally, the prospect wants the job, so he or she will feed you answers that are calculated to win your approval.

Don't ask such difficult questions that the prospect can't possibly answer them. Here are a few questions I think you should avoid:

Why do you want to work here?
What makes you think you're qualified for this job?
Are you interested in this job because of the salary?

Dumb questions like that will make you a rotten interviewer. You must strive to put the prospect at ease so that you can carry on a conversation. Your aim is to know the prospect as a person, and that means avoiding an eyeball-to-eyeball confrontation. Rather, you should make statements or ask questions that will relax the interviewee. If you have to ask a difficult question, wait until the other is at ease, so it doesn't seem so tough.

Mrs. Valencia

"I see by your application, Mrs. Valencia, that one of your hobbies is oil painting. I used to do a little oil painting myself. How did you get started with oil painting as a hobby?"

A question like that accomplished several things. The two of you have something in common. You get Mrs. Valencia talking about herself and her interests. You let her know you're sincerely concerned about her apart from the job. You're interested in her as a person. It's important that you develop that kind of relationship. If this woman is going to work for you, it's the beginning of what could be years of daily contact. And even if she doesn't get the job, she'll feel kindly toward you and your company because you've shown a sincere interest in her.

It's a good idea to spend several minutes talking about the prospect's personal interests before getting around to discussing the job itself. When that time does at last come—and assuming the prospect indeed has a chance for the job—you might consider this approach:

"Mrs. Valencia, before we start talking specifically about the position you've applied for, I'd like to tell you a little about our company. Because, while we're considering you, you're also considering us, so we want to answer any questions you may have about our company." Then go ahead and tell her something about the company. Tell her what your purpose is, but don't spend a lot of time on statistics. Talk more about the company's relationship with its employees. Tell her anything in this area that's unique. You want her to get a feel for the company and its people.

What you're trying to determine is how this prospect's attitudes measure up to what you expect of the person you want in the position.

During the course of this conversation you should be able to determine attitudes. Does the prospect ask questions about the work, the opportunities for promotion, the educational opportunities the company makes available? Or do the questions follow a narrower path? What are the hours? How much vacation do I get? How much sick leave do I get each month?

All these questions may come up during the course of the interview, but what the prospect asks first may give you some clue about her attitude. Be careful not to trigger the order of the questions, however. Eventually during the interview you'll answer all her questions. The idea is to leave the discussion free wheeling enough early in the interview so that the prospect's questions will give you some clue as to what her attitudes are.

You must put the questions in the proper perspective. If the first question asked is about the work schedule and you know the applicant has school-age children, she may be thinking of what she needs in the way of child care. In that case, if the next questions have to do with the work, or with promotional possibilities, then you probably aren't dealing with a person who's concerned only about benefits. That doesn't mean benefits aren't important. They are important. But if you employ people who seem concerned only about what they're going to receive and not at all about what they can contribute, people who aren't particularly interested in knowing whether the job will be challenging or not, it will show up in their performance.

The Married Woman

Years ago, as a young, green manager and long before the women's liberation movement came to national attention, I used to think mothers who needed to work to help meet the family budget requirements made better workers than women not so pressured. How wrong I was! Experience taught me that in many cases these mothers resented having to be away from their children. On the other hand, women who didn't have to work out of financial necessity were at the job because they wanted to be there and as a result they often had a better work attitude.

Not all mothers who had to work resented it, of course, but a great many did. I also saw the same resentment in some young wives who were working to put their husbands through college. It strikes me that the resentment in both situations had to spill over into the marriage and become a potential problem for the couple. This gets back to the one overriding concept about putting people in positions they'll enjoy. They'll do a better job if they like what they're doing and if the work they're doing comes naturally to them.

The Effects of Unemployment Rates

Again concerning unemployment rates, if your town has a high unemployment rate you'll get better acting performances from prospective employees. (If you desperately needed steady work and a steady paycheck, you'd take almost any kind of job. You'd also be more adroit in selling the interviewer on why you should have the job.)

With high unemployment rates, you'll also run into the over-qualified applicant. Frankly, I have mixed emotions about these people. I strongly empathize with them in their current difficulty, but I also realize that once opportunities open up that make it possible for them to cash in on their qualifications, you lose them.

If you can anticipate that opportunities will open up in your company that may suit this over-qualified person, you might be able to retain him or her. I don't know how you can forecast such a situation. If you're desperate for a job, you may be completely honest in telling the interviewer that you intend to stay at your post on a long-term basis. But if you're a trained engineer working at a clerical position, you'd have a tough time convincing yourself that you have an obligation to the company when you're offered a job elsewhere that allows you to return to your own profession.

If you do decide to hire highly over-qualified people, plan on losing them. It's that simple, unless the employees are "comfort zone underachievers."

The Comfort-Zone Underachiever

A comfort-zone underachiever (CZU) is a person who is highly qualified but doesn't like being challenged. There are a lot of them around, but very few admit it.

One of the main problems for CZUs is convincing you they genuinely want to work at a position that seems far below their capacity. They often get burned, in that they're not hired for jobs they want because they're over-qualified. They soon discover that the way to handle this is not to list all their qualifications on the job application. The registered nurse who doesn't want to practice nursing may not indicate her training in that field. She may trim her list of qualifications to fit the clerical job she wants. Likewise, the school-teacher who really can't stand young children in a classroom environment may not list all his credentials. Handling previous work experience on the job application gets more difficult because the trained interviewer will zero in on any gaps. So if our teacher really wants the job as the office "lawn man," his application might show him as a member of the school's "maintenance crew" rather than of its teaching staff.

Since you're interested in getting ahead and managing other people, you may have trouble understanding applicants with this kind of personality. Don't underestimate them. They certainly aren't stupid. They see work from a different perspective than you do. It isn't a matter of who's right and who's wrong. Each attitude is right for the people involved.

It's like the 45-year-old CZU dentist who despised the 19-year-old he once was because of the decision to spend the rest of his life looking into mouths and filling teeth. There are a lot of unhappy people working at unsuitable jobs and we should respect CZUs for having the courage to change their situation. People resist change, and the combination of resisting change and knowing change is necessary leads to inner emotional conflict. I believe that's what psychologists call avoidance–avoidance conflict: you're trapped having to choose between two unpleasant alternatives, because by doing nothing you're eating yourself alive.

The comfort-zone underachiever is trying to find "what's right for me." The job CZUs take may be temporary; they're at a crossroad in a period of reassessment. Often they're looking for a job that won't divert them from their search. The job will require a minimum of attention, thus freeing them to think, to sort things out. Often they'll go after a job that's highly repetitive in nature, that can be done accurately without effort, thus enabling them to daydream. Certain jobs in your own company would doubtless drive you bananas in two hours, but there are people who enjoy doing those jobs; it's a matter of the proper fit.

Work and Play

The word "work" has a bad image for many people. To them, work is a form of punishment. Perhaps it goes back to the ejection of Adam and Eve from the Garden of Eden. If they had not been driven out, they'd have still had to figure out a way to occupy themselves, but the activities would have been by choice and so would have been thought of as play rather than as work. If I play tennis for a living, it's work: but if I play it for recreation, it's play. It's still tennis. Perhaps it comes down to a distinction between "have to" and "want to" situations. That's why many people who are independently wealthy still work. For them it's a "want to" situation.

Mrs. Valencia Again

Let's get back to your interview with your prospective employee, Mrs. Valencia. In talking with her about the job, describe it in nontechnical terms. Use terms that her experience indicates she'll understand. Every business seems to develop a jargon or shorthand that all the experienced employees understand. It may have become so automatic a part of your own vocabulary that you'll have to make a conscious effort to avoid using it. Such jargon is often threatening to a new employee.

It's because of this mumbo jumbo that I have mixed emotions about showing the applicant the job description. If it's written in all this office jargon, it might be better to wait until the new employee is on the job a while.

If you're considering several people for the job, be careful not to mislead any of the prospects. Tell them plainly that several people are being considered. Tell them that only after all the prospects have been interviewed will you make the selection. Never leave them feeling bitter by implying, "don't call us, we'll call you." Tell them when the decision will be made. Then see that they're phoned on that day and informed of the decision.

There are many methods for communicating with people. I prefer that all the prospects be phoned by the personnel department and told that a decision has been made. You might of course want to deliver the good news yourself and phone the person selected. This approach may make you a big shot with Mrs. Valencia, but it won't do a whole lot for your image among people in the personnel department. They handle the dirty work; you handle the good news. If they have to inform nine people that they didn't get the job, the least you can do is let them also bring the good news to the tenth.

The Attitude Talk

After the applicant is selected for the job, you should have your "attitude talk" with the person. I'll give a summary of my own version of an attitude talk; you'll develop your own style after a while, but the basic thoughts will remain the same.

"One of the reasons you were selected for this position is because you display the kind of attitude that we consider essential. Your application and the tests you took indicate that you have the capacity to handle the position. But a lot of people can do the job. It's how they do it that's important to us. We think the difference between an outstanding employee and an average one is a matter of attitude. You'll find both kinds of people in this organization. The attitude we're talking about is one where you aren't worrying about whether or not you're doing more than your share. It's an attitude of pride in doing high-quality work. It's an attitude of accomplishment when the day is done. It's an attitude that tells you you'll benefit more if you can find satisfaction in what you do. We believe you display that kind of attitude, and coupled with your ability to handle the job, that should make you an outstanding addition to our organization."

Now let's analyze the reasons for some of the statements in that minispeech.

When is an employee most likely to be receptive to ideas about the job? I think it's on being hired and on beginning the job.

Do people generally try to live up to the image they think you have of them? I think they do.

Is it imperative to let a new employee know there are people in the organization who are intolerant in certain matters? The bad news will reach the new employee anyway, and sooner than you might expect; your candor will be refreshing.

Is it harmful to suggest to new employees that they should feel a sense of accomplishment at the end of the day? I think not. In fact, the thought might not have occurred to them at all, or as soon, if you had not suggested it.

The exact moment for having your attitude talk with a new employee is a matter of personal preference. I prefer doing it on hiring day, with reinforcement the day the employee starts on the job. This has mainly to do with the nervousness of the employee the first day on the job.

Remember your own first day with a new company. You were probably nervous and apprehensive. You worried about whether your co-workers would like you—or whether you'd like them. You worried about whether you'd catch on quickly enough to the instructions you were given. You worried about looking stupid.

Training the New Employee

In many ways, instructions given employees on their first day are wasted motion. Their first day on the job is an opportunity for new employees to get acquainted with the people they'll be working with and to find out where the rest rooms are. You should permit them to spend the first day just observing, and then start the actual training the second day. Many workers go home from their first day on the job with either a bad headache or a backache—undoubtedly the result of nervous tension.

There are different philosophies on how a person should be trained. The most common holds that a new employee should be trained by the person leaving the job. Automatically following that philosophy can be a mistake. Everything depends on why the employee is leaving, and on his or her attitude.

The Wrong Way: An Example

Let me give an example of the wrong way to train a new employee. It demonstrates the worst kind of judgment I've ever seen displayed in this kind of situation. The manager of an office consisting of several salespeople and one clerical person decided that the clerical person should be fired for incompetence. He gave her two weeks' notice but asked her to work during that time. He then hired her replacement and asked her to train the new employee. The result was a nightmare for all concerned.

And no wonder! If the person leaving your company is less than 100 percent competent, you must never allow him or her to do the training. Most people who put in their notice don't "give a damn" from that point on. The training they do will be casual and incomplete. In addition, they may pass all their bad habits onto the new employee. On the other hand, when a position opens up because the incumbent in the job is being promoted, that person is probably the best one to handle the training.

Concerning the manager who wanted the fired employee to train the replacement, he did not himself understand the clerical job. It was impossible for him personally to train the new employee—any attempt to do so would merely have displayed his ignorance. He therefore went to impossible extremes to "keep his cover." That's a serious managerial failure.

But don't misconstrue what I've said to mean that a manager must personally know how to perform every job in the organization. I don't mean that at all. In the example given, however, there was only one clerical operation. If the manager didn't know that elementary job, how in the world could he effectively manage? The answer is he couldn't!

Managing the Small Office

I've known of situations in small offices with a single secretary and a couple of clerks where the manager takes the attitude, "You handle all of the office routine and the paperwork. I don't care how you do it as long as you get the job done and as long as you can find what I'm looking for."

I don't see how you can manage a small office that way. How do you measure the performance of your subordinate? What is your standard of measurement? Too often people told to do it their own way set out to make themselves indispensable and succeed in the effort.

Unfortunately, that kind of situation prevails in far too many small offices. The clerical staff becomes the office manager and develops systems no one else can figure out. That must not be allowed to occur. The executive in a small office must understand the systems and must forbid any system to develop that enhances the indispensability of subordinates. The system must be the company's and not the employees'.

67

A Solution: The Work Manual

Some companies solve this problem by putting together a work or desk manual that describes the basic office duties and how they're to be performed. Routine, clerical positions lend themselves better to this treatment than more complicated tasks do. Jobs requiring judgment cannot easily be reduced to simple written instructions because all their contingencies cannot be anticipated.

Work manuals are fine if they're kept current. If they're not, they become worthless.

The Role of the Trainer

Before starting a new employee on a training course, you should have a talk with the prospective trainer. You should never spring it as a surprise, so that the first time the trainer learns of the assignment is when you appear on the scene with the new employee in hand. The discussion should take place far enough in advance to permit the trainer to arrange his or her schedule so that the added workload can be accommodated. That may mean reassigning office duties for the duration of the training period.

You must outline to the trainer what you want to happen. If you'd like the first day to be casual, the trainer has to know how you want it handled.

You must continue to display interest in the new employee. Sometime during the latter part of the first day, you should stop by and ask the trainer and the trainee how things are going. What you say isn't important. Your display of interest is what's important.

Another step I recommend is a follow-up talk near the end of the new employee's first week on the job. I'd make this a more formal conversation. I'd call the employee into my office. Again, what is said is not as important as the interest displayed in the new employee's welfare.

A couple of questions, however, should be asked. You should find out if the instructions from the trainer are clear. You should also find out if the new employee is starting to get a handle on the purpose of the job.

The Improvement Seed

This is also the time for planting the *improvement seed.* The process might take this form:

"As a new person on this job you bring fresh insights to the position that the rest of us may not have. After you've been at it a while, you may not be able to see the forest for the trees. I encourage you to ask any questions about what we do and why we do it. After you've been trained, we encourage you to offer any suggestions you can think of to improve what we're doing. Just because you're new doesn't mean your ideas are invalid. What seems obvious to you as a new employee may not be so obvious to the rest of us."

The reason for emphasizing "after you've been trained" is to keep the new employee from suggesting changes before he or she understands what's going on. What may seem like a good idea early in the training may be taken care of as the nature of the position becomes more clearly understood.

Everyone you manage must know that you regularly do this improvement number. In that way you make it less likely that they'll react negatively to new ideas.

You'll always have plenty of problems with people who defend themselves with the statement, "We've always done it this way." Such an argument is usually desperate; it tells you unmistakably that the person using it can't come up with a valid explanation of why something is being done.

The Job Defined

During the training period, it's a good idea to break the job down into small parts and teach the functions one at a time. In showing new employees the entire function you run the risk of overwhelming them. You should of course explain the purpose of the job first.

Feedback

It's important to develop a method of feedback that lets you know how well the trainee is doing after beginning to work unassisted on the job. The trainee should take over the job from the trainer on a gradual basis as each step in the process is mastered. The feedback method should apply to every employee. The system should be developed in such a manner that unsatisfactory performance always comes to your attention before too much damage is done. The process is vital to your success as a manager, but no strict guidelines can be offered for establishing it because it will vary according to the line of business you're in.

The feedback must be internal. Hearing about the mistake from a dissatisfied client or customer means it's already too late. You want to correct the problem before the work gets out of your own area of responsibility.

Quality Control

If it's possible to maintain quality control procedures your employees can relate to, so much the better. Don't expect perfection; that's an unrealistic goal. Determine what an acceptable margin for error should be for your area and then strive as a team to reach that goal and eventually better it. The goal must be realistic if you expect the cooperation of your staff.

A baseball player batting .250 can make out extremely well in the major leagues. One batting .300—getting the job done three times out of ten—is now considered a superstar. You can't survive with that kind of percentage. Depending on what kind of business you're in, it's questionable that you could survive even with a 10 percent rate of error. Let's use a 5 percent rate of error for discussion purposes, even though it may not be realistic for your business.

New employees need to know what's expected of them once they're operating on the job alone. If your ultimate goal for them is 95 percent efficiency, it would help them if they knew what your interim targets are. You might expect them to be working at 70 percent efficiency at the end of 30 days, at 80 percent efficiency at the end of 60 days, and at 95 percent efficiency at the end of 90 days. This will depend on how difficult the work is. The simpler the job, the easier it should be to get to the ultimate quality goal. You have to determine this timetable and let the new employee know what it is.

Even when the new employees take over the job on their own, you should have the trainer audit their work until you believe the work is acceptable and quality checks are not so crucial.

Each mistake should be gone over carefully with the trainee. The trainer should explain what was done wrong, what should have been done, and the reasons. Correcting these mistakes as close to the time of the performance is helpful, because the trainee can probably remember why what was done was done. Every once in a while a mistake will be made that the trainee can't explain. In that case there's nothing to be gained by pressing the matter.

End of the Training Period

A final statement should be made about the training process before we move on to the next chapter. At some point the probationary period must end. In most companies this is usually a specified number of weeks or months. However, I believe that once the trainee demonstrates the ability to work unassisted, it's time for another formal interview between you and the trainee. This marks the completion of a phase in the new employee's career and some attention should be paid to the event. All you really need do is express your satisfaction about the progress made up to this point, note that the employee will now be working on his or her own, and indicate how the work will be monitored both for quality and for quantity.

9

"Oh my God, I can't fire anyone!"

If there's one moment that will live forever in a manager's memory, it's the first time a subordinate had to be fired. It's not a pleasant task. If you enjoy it, then I question your ability to manage people.

Firing someone can be traumatic for both parties in the drama. If you've done your job properly, the event will not come as a surprise to the person who is about to get the ax.

Impetuous firings must never take place. Never fire someone when you're angry. Never take such radical action on an impulse. When a subordinate pushes you "over the edge" and you feel like "showing him who's boss," don't give in to your emotions. If you do, you'll regret it.

As you read this chapter the thought may occur to you that some people don't deserve the time and consideration I'm recommending you use. You may be right, but I believe in erring on the side of excess deliberation than on the side of excess haste. In fact, a philosophy some managerial friends of mine have used is never to fire a subordinate until everyone in the office is wondering why you haven't taken the step already.

Preparing the Ground for the Divorce

Documentation of the troublesome employee's performance is critically important. Of course, you must keep such records for all your employees. If your company has a formal performance appraisal system, then you may be adequately covered.

Records are important because being sued for dismissing an employee is becoming more common. You should ask yourself, "If I have to, can I fully justify this dismissal?" If you can answer yes, that's all you need worry about.

Many supervisors agonize over every situation where they've had to let someone go. I prefer that a supervisor care too much than be completely callous about it.

Most of the firing situations don't develop overnight. Perhaps I've been extremely fortunate in my managerial life, but I've never had to fire anyone for getting into a fight and smacking someone in the mouth. That kind of situation, along with committing an office crime like stealing, clearly doesn't lend itself to my concept of "no surprise firings." Such situations are no doubt covered by company policy.

The more typical kinds of discharge that you're likely to run into in your managerial career have to do with poor performance and the employee's inability or unwillingness to abide by the company's standards. Some people will never be able to cut the job. They may get to a satisfactory training performance level but will never advance beyond that point to the performance level the job requires.

Firing is not the first thought that should come into your head. You must first satisfy yourself that the training has been correct and clearly understood. Was there any kind of personality barrier between the trainer and the trainee that impeded the flow of adequate information? Go back over the employee's aptitude tests, job application, and other initial hiring data on the chance that you may have missed something. Only after you're completely convinced that you have a below-satisfactory performer with little or no hope of bringing the performance up to proper standards should you consider termination as a possible solution.

Has the new employee been told that his or her performance is not up to the standard that is expected? You owe it to your people to let them know what the situation is. And that includes telling them when they're performing well. Too many managers assume that if employees don't get bad performance reports, they know they're doing okay. I've got news for you. Those employees believe you "don't give a damn"—and I think they're right on target.

A False Sense of Superiority

This may be the right place to suggest that too many executives believe they're more intelligent than the people working for them. That may not be true. If you have the attitude that subordinate is a synonym for inferior, you're not ready for management, in my opinion. Unfortunately, business is populated with executives who feel that way, and the quality of their leadership suffers constantly from it. I don't know how you get managers with that attitude to change it; perhaps the experience of a few failures is the only way.

Some executives feel they have to be smarter than all their subordinates. It'll never work. The successful executive is willing to hire people who are more competent in certain areas than he or she is. They'll actually make your job easier and help prepare you for additional promotion.

A Second Chance

Getting back to the employee whose job performance is

unsatisfactory, you of course handle it in such a way that the employee knows you're addressing yourself to the work and not to the person. At some point in the conversation you let the employee know that termination will come if the performance standards cannot be met. But it's not enough to let it go at that. Set a target for the employee to reach, in terms both of work improvement and of a time to achieve the goal. You have to be specific. "You're now averaging ten errors each day. You'll have to cut this down to three errors each day by the end of two weeks." Your precise specifications serve a dual purpose. If the employee meets the goal, you may be on the way to solving the problem and retaining the employee. Failing that, you're ready to start the termination process.

Is it possible that this employee could handle some other job in your own area that is currently available? Or if an opening is coming up in accounting, can the employee make a contribution? Is this a situation where a person has been hired for the wrong job? Does the company gain anything by firing someone who might be useful somewhere else? Will the employee be so embarrassed by what appears to be failure that the stigma will carry over into future jobs? Is your company large enough that the employee could be moved to another area with no stigma? Former employees are part of a company's public. Can you handle the situation in such a way that you don't subtract from your company's storehouse of civic goodwill? Even though the employee won't like being fired, can you handle the procedure so that the employee will admit to having been given every opportunity, and will consequently agree that you had no choice in the matter?

Right here let me warn against taking the coward's way out and blaming the mysterious *they*. "As far as I'm concerned, ten errors a day isn't too bad, but *they* say we have to

get it down to three, or *they* will force me to let you go."
That indicates you're merely a puppet. Someone else is pulling the strings. You don't have a mind of your own.

You have to level with the employee who is not measuring up. I know of managers who surgarcoat all bad news to such an extent that the employee on the receiving end feels complimented on having done a clearly outstanding job.

Flexibility and Consistency

Some of your people will also need to be dismissed because of poor attendance. Companies have such a wide variety of sick-leave programs, however, that it's impossible to discuss what level of absenteeism is satisfactory. I personally don't care for sick-leave programs that allow, for example, one sick day per month or twelve per year, cumulatively. I prefer a method that allows supervisory discretion based on the individual situation. For example, I can decide not to dock a good loyal employee for a day's absence. I can also decide that an employee with a bad attendance record has abused the privilege and must consequently be docked for a day's absence.

Admittedly, this kind of program is more difficult to administer than one with hard and fast rules to follow. In making decisions on the merits of each case, you have to be able to defend your decisions.

One disadvantage in having no formal program is the serious risk that decisions will not be made consistently throughout the company. In some departments, a generous executive will excuse almost any absence and pay the absentee; other managers may be more strict and dock for days missed. Having no formal program means the communication between departments and executives has to be extremely good, ensuring that approximately the same standards apply throughout the company.

The Dismissal Drama

So far we've discussed events leading up to a dismissal. Now let's talk about the dismissal itself. I'm referring to a dismissal whose timing you control.

My preference has always been to stage the drama on late Friday afternoon. By the time it's over, all the co-workers of the person being fired will have left the office. Thus, the dismissed employee won't have to endure the humiliation of "clearing out" in front of an audience. In addition, the coming weekend can be used to pull things together and prepare for seeking other employment, applying for unemployment compensation, or whatever else is to be done.

Any money due at the time of the dismissal should be given to the dismissed employee at the end of the interview. Being canned is enough of an emotional blow; wondering when the final check will arrive can only add to the misery. Severance pay—if that's the company's policy—should be given at the same time. Unused vacation time or sick leave should also be included in the compensation.

Put yourself in the other's position. You're not going to feel the termination was completely justified. Unless you receive every dollar you have coming to you, you'll probably think, "Well, I suppose I'll have to hire an attorney to get the money this chicken outfit owes me!" Remove that thought from the dismissed employee's mind by taking care of all those matters in advance.

Another courtesy that I think you owe the employee is to keep your intention to fire him or her as confidential as possible. Of course, the personnel department will have to know, and the payroll department. But other than the necessary management people you discuss it with, the matter should be treated on a confidential basis.

The final scene in the dismissal drama is bound to be the most uncomfortable for the supervisor. Because in that highly charged interview it's just the two of you face to face and you want to get it over with as quickly as possible.

A good way to start is to review in brief what has happened. Don't drag it out and make it a recitation of all of the other's mistakes. I prefer something like this: "As you know from our past conversations, we had certain standards on the job that had to be met. I think we approached reaching those standards on a fair and reasonable basis. As I've mentioned to you from time to time over the past few weeks, you haven't been able to meet those standards. I don't believe it's because of any lack of effort on your part. However, it hasn't worked out, and I don't think that comes as any surprise to you. But we're going to have to terminate your services as of today. I really regret that. I wanted it to work out just as much as you did. But it hasn't worked out, and so we have to face up to reality. Here's the final check, plus one month's severance pay, plus your unused vacation and sick-leave time. This should give you a continuation of income for a time sufficient for you to find another job."

You can vary your remarks to fit the individual situation, but I think the above words say what needs to be said. They don't sugarcoat the bad news, I don't think they're too blunt either. You have to come up with a statement that fits the situation, and one you're comfortable with.

I assume there are no more companies that fire people by putting a pink slip in their pay envelope. That's inhumane, in my opinion. I can understand the necessity for it in a factory where thousands of people are all being temporarily laid off. I can also understand using the method if the entire business is being closed and everybody is going. Situations like that are not related to the performance of the individual. When someone is being let go because of a personal failure to perform or live up to company standards, the only way to handle it is on a one-on-one basis. The manager might prefer to avoid the direct confrontation, but it's part of the job's responsibilities and must be dealt with straight on.

When you consider it thoughtfully, you realize that keeping an unsatisfactory employee on the job is unfair not only to the company but also to the employee. No one is comfortable in a job he or she is not performing well.

I recall a situation a number of years ago where being canned turned out to be the biggest favor ever done for that young man. He was trying to function in an accounting position but was not cutting the mustard. After being let go, he decided to continue his education. He entered a law college and is now practicing his profession very successfully.

I find that people avoid the word "fire" as they do the word "die." They say, "pass away," "go on to his reward," "cross over." Instead of "fire" they say, "dismiss," "discharge," "let go," "canned."

One last thought: you must be absolutely certain in your own mind that the firing is deserved. You must be sure you're being as objective as you can possibly be. If in doubt, use a more experienced executive as a sounding board. Then when you know you have to fire the employee, make sure it doesn't come as a surprise. And handle it in a considerate, humane, and delicate manner.

The manager
as administrator
and counselor

Your relationship with the personnel department

How much you interact with your company's personnel department will depend on how much latitude you're allowed in the selection process. In many companies the personnel department does the initial screening of prospective employees, but the final decision on hiring is left to the appropriate manager.

It's my belief that the overall selection process is strengthened if the final choice is made at the operating level. If a manager had nothing to say about the person hired and is unhappy with the choice, the new employee won't have the same chance for being successful. Fortunately, most companies do allow the operating department to make the final selection from several qualified candidates.

Although people working in personnel consider themselves experts on selecting employees, it doesn't matter who they think is the best qualified if the person is someone you don't want. How you react to the personnel department's recommendation is important. You must take their recommendations seriously. This assumes that through talks with you they fully understand what the job requires. If they don't it's because you haven't given them the information they need. They can't be experts on every job in the company, even with access to all the job descriptions. You're the expert on the jobs in your area of responsibility, and you ought to know what's required.

You'll also become involved with the personnel department in the promotion area. Most of the time you'll try to promote employees from within your own area, but there'll be times when you'll need to look to other areas of the company for the staff you need and the people in personnel will be in a position to help you. For example, they can show you the original data collected when the person was hired, which might include scores from aptitude tests given at the time. In most cases, they'll consult with the department that employs your potential promotee and get important information you might not have gotten on your own.

Also, in some companies the personnel department is used for administering employee benefit programs, and so you could be going to them on behalf of subordinates who are having difficulties with some aspect of the program.

If you haven't managed people before, personnel can be a strong resource for you. You can usually go to them for advice and counsel on supervisory problems you've never encountered before. The personnel department is also the usual repository for books on the management of people.

In many companies, the personnel department handles the education and training of managers. Since the department serves a staff function to the entire company, you can often talk with someone there about "people problems" that you might be reluctant to discuss with your own superior. So you can look to personnel for assistance not only in selecting people but also in managing them.

I know of organizations that use the personnel department as a place where employees can go with any problems they don't wish to discuss with their own boss. This can be a valuable service both to the employees and to the company. It is hoped that your personnel department has been properly trained and educated in its function.

One or two visits to the chief of the personnel department should give you an indication of what help you can expect. You ought to cultivate a strong working relationship with everyone in the department.

Job descriptions, performance appraisals, and salary administration

These are functions every company performs, either formally or informally. They're useful procedures, but because the people administering them are not properly instructed in what their purpose is, they're often mismanaged.

We have to speak of these functions from a conceptual viewpoint. Discussion of such precise details as the forms used is unfeasible because of the great variation in approaches that exists between industries and even between companies within individual industries.

Even companies without a formal program use such techniques—although often poorly. Informality is more likely to be found in smaller companies that are family controlled, or where one or two people make all the decisions. Such autocrats may feel they're being equitable and that all the employees are satisfied with the fair treatment they're receiving; that may indeed be the case; but the chances for it are remote. Even without a formal program, someone in charge decides which jobs are most important (job evaluation), makes a judgment on how well people are doing, (performance appraisal), and decides how much each employee is going to be paid (salary administration). So even if the motto is, "We're all like one happy family and as papa I make all the decisions based on what's fair," the company does have a program—with all the idiosyncratic biases of the "papa" thrown in.

Job Descriptions

Many companies use job descriptions, although they may be called something else. A list of job descriptions should not be confused with a desk manual that tells not only exactly what has to be done on the job but also exactly how to do it. A job description, rather, tells *what* is done.

The information required for a job description will vary widely, depending on what consulting service your company is using, but certain bits of information seem common to the job descriptions of most services. Besides telling what is done, a typical job description usually indicates what educational background is required, how much experience is needed before a trainee in the position can be called a fully trained incumbent, what the specific accountabilities of the position are, and the extent of the supervisory responsibility.

Some methods of describing jobs will require spelling out specific objectives that are both short term and long term. The relationship of the person in the job to other people in the organization will often be covered. For example, what position does the job report to? What people does the job require contacting? Who are those people in the organization? The description may also indicate whether the job requires contacts with the public, either in person or by telephone. All these factors may become important in evaluating the job and determining where the position fits in the overall job hierarchy.

At some point you'll have the opportunity to write a job description either for yourself or for subordinates. Some companies allow managers to write their own job description and others require that the description be written by the immediate supervisor of the job. I believe it's best if the descriptions are written jointly by the employee and the supervisor, so that both are in agreement as to what the job is. A great deal of mental anguish and ineffectual performance can perhaps be avoided in that way.

As to the actual writing of the description itself, it's best not to use a lot of boiler-plate copy. Also, puffing up the job to make it sound impressive usually works to your disadvantage. If a scoring committee has to go through the ordeal of sifting out the facts from all the hokum, it could result in the job being ranked lower than it deserves to be.

Of course you want a job in your area—and your own job —to score as highly as possible in the organization, but the job's actual duties will have to justify the scoring. If it were possible to determine the importance of jobs by overwriting their functions, then you wouldn't have the proper relationship between jobs within the organization. The best jobs would be those that were most effectively inflated by the writer describing them. That's in no one's best interest, because no matter how good you are at puffery, there'll always be someone who's better. Stick with the facts!

Performance Appraisals

Performance appraisals can be as informal as telling someone, "You've done a nice job," or as elaborate as a full-scale written report, complete with a long follow-up interview with the employee.

Clearly all of us like to know how we're doing. One employee will say "working in this office is like working in the dark." Another will say "One thing about old Fussbudget, he may be tough, but you always know where you stand." It's meant as a compliment.

A formal system of performance appraisal—for example, one or two planned contacts with the employee each year for the specific purpose of discussing "how you're doing"—is preferable to the informal method, which is often equivalent to doing nothing.

Some managers are convinced that they communicate effectively with their employees and that these employees know exactly how they stand. An interview with the employees, however, will indicate that communication is one of the greatest needs they feel.

Too many executives still approach their supervisory role with the motto, "If they don't hear anything, they know they're doing okay." That doesn't cut it. Top-echelon managers too often avoid discussing all performances except those that require emergency action. They feel that, whereas performance appraisals are necessary for the rank and file, members of the executive team are above such things. The rationale is that these officials are clearly in control of the situation and themselves and don't need to be told how they're doing. Just the opposite is true. Members of the executive team may have an even greater need to be told how their performance is viewed by their superiors. One reason is that there's often much greater ego need at this level.

The Appraisal Form

A formal system should be designed in such a way that it considers as many elements of the job as possible. The manager should be forced to make some judgment about each of the important factors. This means, first of all, that the executive must be knowledgeable about the job and the performance. That's why the appraisal should be done at the level closest to the job being reviewed. A manager three levels above the position in question can't handle the judgments as well as the manager in daily contact with the employee being appraised. It can be reviewed by higher-level management, but the appraisal will be more accurate when done by someone in daily contact with the job.

Here are some items that appear on a typical performance appraisal form. There may be anywhere from three to ten degrees of performance efficiency for each category, the extremes being "unsatisfactory" on the one end and "outstanding" on the other.

Volume or production levels
Thoroughness
Accuracy
Initiative or attitude
Ability to learn
Cooperation
Attendance and punctuality

You can probably think of other factors applying to your own business that ought to be included. Some systems may use a numeric weighting for each of the factors, arriving at a final rating that will be given to the employee. The entire form becomes a part of the employee's personnel file. The ranking scheme might be something like this:

80 to 100 points—Outstanding
60 to 80 points—Commendable
50 to 60 points—Satisfactory
40 to 50 points—Needs improvement
Less than 40 points—Unsatisfactory

The ranges can be narrower if your system is designed that way. Some companies may consider anything below 70 points as unsatisfactory.

The Interview

The interview with the employee about the performance appraisal becomes crucial. You should plan to hold it at a time when you'll be unhurried and not likely to be interrupted. Allow yourself as much time as is needed to cover all facets of the job. Answer all questions. Listen to everything the employee wants to say. Your willingness to hear your subordinate out may be as important as the discussion itself. Employees are so used to dealing with managers who behave as though everything is an emergency that, when given time to talk to their superior about their own dreams and aspirations, they feel uncomfortable.

The conversation with your subordinate is so important that you should instruct your secretary to hold your telephone calls. This should include even calls from the president of the company. Of course, anyone in any organization can be interrupted for emergencies, but you should not take phone calls of a routine nature. It's quite disconcerting to be telling another about your ambitions and feelings only to have the other break the spell by taking several phone calls.

We're slaves to the telephone to an extent that's difficult to understand. How many times have you been outside the door and gone rushing back into the house to answer the phone only to find it's a magazine salesman? Somehow, there's an urgency about a telephone ringing that demands response.

I once read about an elderly gentleman who had what I consider the ideal attitude toward the telephone. One evening, while he was chatting with a neighbor over his backyard fence, his telephone could be heard ringing inside his house. The man serenely disregarded the incessant summons, until his neighbor could stand it no longer and said with some irritation in his voice, "Aren't you going to get that phone?" The man replied, "No, I put that telephone in for *my* convenience." That would indeed seem the correct attitude to take toward Mr. Bell's invention.

Getting back to the performance appraisal interview, you should direct the tone of the discussion but not dominate it. You definitely have a message to convey. You want to go over each performance appraisal factor with your subordinate. You want to make known what you consider to be your subordinate's strengths on the job and which areas require some improvement. You'll seldom get disagreement on the areas you designate as strengths. Where you're likely to encounter disagreement is when you get around to discussing weaknesses. And this is where you have to allow the employee to express his or her own feelings.

Do you have documentation that indicates where the employee is weak and where improvement is needed? Your case is much stronger if buttressed by hard evidence. Production or quality records are much more convincing than an executive's intuition. When you come up against the subordinate's disagreement, that difference of opinion is important and should be discussed. It's possible that you're wrong, but you won't be if the facts can be documented.

An experiment I once engaged in was a great help to me in getting my staff to understand performance appraisals. Before sitting down to make my Solomon-like judgments, I gave all the members of my staff a blank form and asked them to evaluate their own performance. We then compared their appraisals with mine; with only one exception, their ratings were lower than mine. I'm not a liberal grader, so that wasn't the reason. We were then able to discuss our views of each factor rated. They learned a great deal about performance appraisal from the experiment, but I learned a great deal more about the people I was managing.

Too many leaders will be thorough in pointing out the areas in which the employee should show improvement, but they will not go far enough. If they're going to tell the employee where job performance is not up to expectations, then they must also tell *how* it can be improved. This needs to be thought through in great detail before the interview is even held.

The Agenda

This brings us to the preparation time that I believe is essential to a successful performance appraisal interview. You should sit down and decide what points you want to cover in the conversation. You might even prepare a brief outline of what you want to discuss. It's possible that the performance appraisal form your company uses may trigger all the proper thoughts in your mind. However, you must anticipate that it will not. You'll look quite foolish if you fail to cover all the bases and have to ask the employee to come back into your office a day later to cover some important point that you forgot.

I recommend that you actually make an outline of the significant items you should cover. Here are some questions you might ask yourself as you prepare the outline:

—What areas of this employee's performance or attitude should I mention?

—What areas not covered in the performance appraisal do I need to mention?

—What are some of the items of personal interest about this employee that I should bring up?

—What questions should I ask this employee that are likely to generate some conversation and opinions about the work?

—How can I help this employee do a better job? What are the areas in which this employee will be self-motivated?

—How can I let this employee know he or she is important to me personally, and not just for the work
performed?
—How does this employee fit into the company's future
plans? Is this person promotable? What can I do to
help?

I'm sure you get the idea of the kind of self-examination
you should go through before beginning the session with
the employee. A few minutes spent preparing for the conversation will greatly increase the success ratio of your performance appraisal interviews.

The Satisfactory Employee

Many executives prepare quite thoroughly for the interview with the problem employee. They know it might get
sticky and they'd better see to it that their flanks are pro-
tected. You should be just as thorough in preparing for the
interview with the satisfactory employee. You'll be suprised
occasionally by the outstanding staff member who'll turn a
conversation that you thought was going to be all
"sweetness and light" into a real donnybrook.

As you spend more years in management you'll find that
the satisfactory employee generally uses this interview to
unload some of the problems that have been festering. The
problems vary with the situation. Here are some examples:

I'm not advancing fast enough.
My salary is not fair for the work I do.
My co-workers are not performing up to standards.
As manager, you don't pay enough attention to subordi-
nates who are getting the job done.
Good performance is not appreciated or recognized.

You should welcome such input from your satisfactory
employees, even though you risk hearing what you don't

want to hear. Let's face it, many employees will tell you only what they think you want to hear, but a rare and precious few will be truth-tellers,and these you must listen carefully to. Don't fall into the "shoot the messenger" syndrome. Although the news a messenger brings you makes you unhappy, the fault is not with the messenger; punishing the carrier won't change the truth of the message carried. Ignorance may be bliss, but it can be fatal in a managerial career.

Of course, the information you're receiving may not exactly reflect the facts. But even though you're receiving it through the carrier's filters, that doesn't make it any less valuable. You've been around long enough to know how to sort out what's important and what's window dressing. If the satisfactory employee believes it's important enough to bring to your attention, then you ought to listen to it. Besides, this subordinate surely knows you prefer a trouble-free interview to one filled with problems, so you know the matter would not have come up unless the man or woman felt strongly about it.

It's possible that you may occasionally have a mischief-maker on your hands, but such people are usually not your highly satisfactory employees.

An Open Door Policy

"My door is always open." How many times have you said it yourself? It doesn't take the employees long to find out what the statement really means.

"My door is always open, as long as you don't come in here to tell me about any new problems." That's one possible meaning. "My door is always open, but don't come in to talk about money or a better job." That's another. "My door is always open, but I don't want to hear about your personal problems." Your employees know what you really mean or they soon figure it out.

Your performance appraisal interviews should encourage

your subordinates to say whatever they have in mind. The more open the communication between you, the better chance that you'll have a satisfactory working relationship.

Salary Administration

It should be pretty obvious that job descriptions, performance appraisals, and salary administration all fit together in one overall plan. They're designed to provide accurate descriptions of what people do, give fair evaluations of their performance, and pay them a salary that's reasonable for their effort. All these factors must bear a proper relationship to one another and make a contribution to the organization's overall goals.

If you have a job evaluation program, you probably also have salary ranges for each position in the organization. As a manager, you work within that scale. Such a system usually includes a range of pay increases you can recommend based on the kind of performance appraisal the employee has received. Since the two procedures have such an impact on each other, some companies separate the performance appraisal rating from the salary recommendation. In that way a supervisor's idea of what a salary increase ought to be is not allowed to determine the performance appraisal given. If as supervisor you make both determinations at the same time, you'll be tempted to take the answer you want and work backward to justify it. It remains difficult to separate salary consideration from the performance appraisal, but completing the procedures several weeks or months apart may help.

So let's assume your company does have salary ranges for each job and there's some limitation on what you can recommend. No doubt the salary ranges overlap. For example, a veteran employee on a lower-level job could be paid more than a newer employee on a higher-level job. Or an out-standing performer at one level could be paid more than a mediocre worker one level up.

Equity

As the manager, you're concerned with equity. You should review the salaries of all the people who report to you. You might begin by listing all the jobs in your depart-ment, from top to bottom. You might then write the monthly salary behind each name. Based on what you know about the job performances, do the salaries look reasonable? Is there any salary that looks out of line?

Another method you can use is to rank the jobs in the order of importance to the department, as you perceive the situation. How does that compare with top management's evaluation of the importance of the jobs? If there are differ-ences you can't reconcile or accept, then you'd better sched-ule a session with your immediate superior to see what can be done about it.

In this matter of rankings, appraisals, and salaries, a word of caution is in order. Recognize, and be willing to admit to yourself, that you like some employees more than others. You're conning yourself if you think you like them all equally. Certain personality types are more agreeable to you than others. Try as honestly as you can to keep these person-ality preferences from unduly influencing the decisions you make about appraisals, salaries, and promotions.

In recommending salary increases for several subordi-nates, you'll have some tricky decisions to make. If the com-pany makes all its salary adjustments at the same time each year, then it's fairly easy to compare one recommendation against another. You can make all your decisions at one time and see how they stack up with one another. But if salary decisions are spread throughout the year—for example, as when tied to the worker's employment anniversary—it's then more difficult to have all the decisions spread out in front of you.

Maintaining equity in this type of situation, although difficult, can be achieved if you keep adequate records. Retain copies of all your job descriptions, performance appraisals, and salary recommendations. Some companies encourage supervisors not to keep such records and to depend on the personnel department's records. I believe that maintaining your own set is worth the effort; you'll then have them when you want them.

The Salary Recommendation

In making a salary recommendation, be as sure as you possibly can be that it's a reasonable amount. It should be neither too low nor too high, while at the same time fitting within the framework of the performance the company is receiving from that person. An increase that's too high, for example, could create an "encore" problem. Anything less than the same amount offered the next time around may be considered an insult by the employee. However, an unusually large increase coming at the time of a promotion doesn't run that same encore danger, because it can be tied to a specific, nonrepeating yearly situation. In that case, you must explain to the employee why the increase is so large and why it doesn't create a precedent for future increases.

Since a small increase can be considered an insult, you'd perhaps do better to recommend no increase at all rather than a pittance. Sometimes a small increase is a cop-out and is given because the supervisor lacks the courage to recommend no increase. But this only postpones the inevitable reckoning; I recommend confronting it immediately and honestly.

When considering the amount of the raise, it's essential that you not allow the employee's need to be an important factor. Before assuming I'm being inhumane, consider these points. If you based salary increases on need, the employee in the most desperate state of need would be the highest paid. If that person is also the best performer, you'd have no problem, but what if the employee's performance is merely average?

The company may also want to recognize the length of time an employee has spent with the organization, but the common thread that must run through salary administration is merit. Basing your salary recommendations on who has the greatest number of children, or whose mother is ill, moves you away from your responsibilities as a salary administrator and puts you in the charity business. If you have subordinates with such financial problems, you can be helpful as a friend, a good listener, or a source of information about where to go for professional assistance, but you can't use the salary dollars you're charged with as a method of solving the social problems of your subordinates.

Many companies now have employee assistance programs. These are designed either to help such people out of temporary problems or to direct them to professional help should that be necessary. When you're making a salary adjustment for a subordinate who's having difficulty, there's a great temptation to add a few more dollars than you would otherwise. You must resist that temptation and base your decision strictly on the performance of the individual employee.

12

Is there such a thing as motivation?

"I'm going to get you to do what I want you to do—and like it. But even if you don't like it, you'll do it—and the way I want it done." Basically, that's how a great many managers view the subject of motivation, as a polite word for describing the proper use of authority.

At one time a psychological consulting firm was working in our office. During a feedback session the psychologist assigned to me commented that I was reluctant to use the power of my position to get things done and that I was more interested in persuading people. He meant it as constructive criticism, but I accepted it as a compliment and still do.

I believe one of the greatest strengths of a leader is his or her ability to get the job done without having to reach back and use the power of the position. I know it's there. I can always reach back and use it if I have to, but isn't the power of the position just as strong if I don't use it? Doesn't my use of the power mean I'm desperate, unable to achieve my objectives in any other way? Clearly, it's more of a resource when I don't use it.

100

Self-Motivation

The only motivation that really works is self-motivation. When you do a job because you want to, your motivation is self-perpetuating. You don't have to be bludgeoned into doing it. One of the primary responsibilities of a manager is to change the feelings of subordinates from "have to" to "want to."

Also a good manager gets the job done by finding out how different people respond. If they're self-motivated, they're self-motivated either to get the job done or to just get by. They react in different ways, and you need to understand them well enough to know how they react and to what.

Some people are self-motivated by the possibility of a promotion. As soon as they see a relationship between their current performance and a promotion, they'll strive to perform at the top of their efficiency. Others seek their manager's approval. Since satisfactory performance is how they receive the approval, that's the route they follow. Still others like to compete in a friendly way with their peers. They want to be the best performer in the area and so will work hard at achieving that objective.

Many people are working simply for the dollar, and the way to get more dollars is to perform well to maximize the next salary increase. Many others take great personal pride in doing whatever they do well. Depending on the condition of the labor market, a number will be working hard to keep from being unemployed—although this doesn't seem to be a strong factor any more.

Some workers bring their feeling for family into their attitude toward the job, but that's often tied in turn to one of the other reasons I've mentioned—pursuing the dollar. They want to be able to provide more for the family, which requires more dollars.

The Manager's Role

You'll find that learning how to maximize the performance of your people is a permanent, ongoing part of your daily business life. Unless you're in an unusual situation, you'll have turnover, and turnover brings in new people who must be understood. Your obligation in this matter deserves particular emphasis. Your people want to be understood by you. They want to feel important to you as a person —not just as a piece of machinery for getting the work done. Your genuine concern for them will shine through all you do. You don't have to become a father figure in order to assure them that you understand them and appreciate them. And you don't have to compromise your principles as far as the quality of work is concerned.

Too many managers have the mistaken idea that if you care for your people and understand them, that somehow subtracts from the quality of the work; it indicates a softness or weakness in you that your subordinates will exploit; it must end eventually in your losing control. Just because you care for them and are interested in their well-being, however, doesn't mean that your people don't have to perform on the job. Concern for and understanding of your staff are signs of management strength, not weakness. The tough, autocratic leader may get satisfactory results for a while, but over the long haul the destroyer will inevitably become the destroyed.

Too many managers believe you can't be fair, concerned, and understanding and still be tough when the situation requires it. You can be. Being fair, concerned, and understanding will make it easier to be tough when the situation demands it. Many managers think that if they're too understanding, they'll be tempted to "cave in" every time a request is made of them. It need not work that way.

In order to establish a proper rapport with your people you have to get to know them. Getting to know them is often a long, ongoing process because of the changes that will occur in personnel and because even the long-term employees' circumstances will change. Because of such changing circumstances, they'll react differently at various phases of their career.

Oftentimes managers will get the idea that they need be concerned only about new employees. An employee brought up to a satisfactory level of performance can be disregarded. This is a mistake. If you don't pay attention to the more seasoned employees, you'll develop problems. The seasoned employee who is doing a satisfactory job will resent being ignored. If you pay attention only to your problem areas, you'll soon find that problems are arising in areas where you didn't expect them. People simply don't like being taken for granted. They need proper care and attention.

Don't imagine you can eventually learn all that needs to be done in this area of self-motivation. There's always more to learn because of the immense variety of personalities you'll meet on the job. I know of a manager who once told a subordinate that he had a great need for recognition, but who then refused to give the man that recognition because it would presumably have been considered a sign of weakness.

What was wrong, in the first place, was telling the subordinate there was a great need for recognition, as though that was a shortcoming. Telling a person that there's a great need for recognition as though it's a fault is counterproductive to what the objective ought to be. The manager's objective ought to be to increase the effectiveness of the subordinate and increase his or her feeling of contribution and well-being.

The Role Played by Titles

This brings me to the subject of titles in an office. Nearly every industry has titles that are peculiar to it and that may not be meaningful to people unfamiliar with the industry. Their significance to people within the industry should not be underestimated.

I've always maintained that titles don't cost a company anything and that you ought to be liberal in using them so long as you can maintain some equity within your organization. By such liberality you not only give recognition to your people but help give them some status within their own community.

The banking industry is well known for this practice, and although some executives in other businesses put them down for it, I think the banks know exactly what they're doing. A customer of a bank dealing with the "Vice President—Consumer Loans" will feel much more gratified than if dealing with a "Loan Clerk." The spouse of the "Vice President—Consumer Loans" is surely a greater booster of the bank than the spouse of the "Loan Clerk." In every possible way, the bank's standing in the community is elevated by this liberality with its titles.

The strange thing is that the vice president in this instance may have the same duties as the loan clerk. But which has the more positive self-image and the stronger self-motivation? The answer is obvious.

As you move up the corporate ladder you may be in a position to influence your company's policy on the use of titles. I sincerely believe you'll get a lot more "house" from and for your entire employee group if you use the more liberal approach. Giving someone a title doesn't cost you one thin dime.

Of course, you handle these titles in an orderly fashion. You don't start a new employee off with a super title for a routine position. Rather, the title is out there for the employee to aspire to and achieve in a reasonable length of time.

Show me a company that's parsimonious in its title policy and I'll show you a company with a management team whose morale can be increased dramatically by a more enlightened use of titles. Its impact will be positive even on those who are not yet a part of the management team, because they'll see what it's possible for them to achieve.

There's nothing wrong with making people feel good about their position and its importance to the organization. Titles can often go a long way toward giving an employee that sense of well-being. I'm amazed at how shortsighted some executives can be on this subject.

An example taken from below the managerial level would be the secretary of a company executive. Instead of calling the position "Secretary," what's wrong with calling it "Executive Secretary?" Which title is the employee more likely to prefer? Some executives don't want to call the position "Executive Secretary" because that would give the employee too inflated a sense of importance. Executives should worry more about making people feel *properly* important than about making them feel *too* important. We all want to feel important, including our employees. Let's help them experience that feeling.

The Status Symbol

Another matter that falls in the motivation area is the status symbol. Obviously, status symbols work or they wouldn't find so widespread an application in the business world.

The key to the executive washroom has almost become a joke. I don't understand how anybody can be turned on about this, but perhaps I don't understand the washroom psychology. The size of the office, the luxuriousness of the carpeting, wooden versus steel furniture, executive parking privileges, an executive dining room, company-paid club memberships, company-leased automobiles for executive use, corporate aircraft—the proliferation of status symbols is limited only by the expansiveness of the human imagination.

All could be considered as attempts to inspire people to raise their aspirations. These things are not important in themselves, but indicate that the employee is recognized as having arrived at a certain level in the organization. They're a lot more important to those who don't have them than to those who do. As a friend of mine says about money, "Why is it that most of the people who say money isn't important are just the ones who have plenty of it?" The same goes for status symbols.

A company should not become overly concerned about status symbols, but if it makes them available to its employees it should not then criticize those same employees for longing after these "methods of keeping score." Actually, for most people, it's not the acquisition of the symbols that's important; it's what they signify to other people. Most status symbols would fall by the wayside if no one else knew you had achieved them.

It's fine to want to achieve certain status symbols, but it's important that you keep them in proper perspective. Don't let them become so critical to you that it'll tear you up if you don't achieve them as quickly as you think you should.

An item I read in *Business Week* perhaps captures the flavor of the point I'm trying to get across about motivation and self-motivation. An article written about a union convention dealt with the attitudes of younger people in the union; its essence was contained in the sentence, "Young workers demand better treatment on the job, and they are equally angry about 'authoritarian bosses' in the plants and 'unresponsive bureaucrats' in the unions." Later in the story, a 25-year-old union member is quoted as saying, "You should be treated as a man first, and a worker second."

That strong feeling is shared by most people, no matter where they are in an organization. Not only do your subordinates want you to treat them in that manner, but I'm sure it's the way you want them to behave toward you. It's not an unreasonable request. It's also sound management.

13

Helping prepare for the gold watch

Although helping people prepare for retirement is a company-wide responsibility, your involvement as their supervisor is crucial to prospective retirees because you represent the company to them to a large extent. You're involved in managing their day-to-day activities and you therefore have the greatest contact with them.

The thought may occur to you that it's a bit odd to be talking about retirement in a book aimed at the new manager. It would indeed be odd if we were talking about your own retirement, but since it could happen at any time to someone under your supervision, you must be prepared for it.

I would even suggest that you start associating with someone close to retirement on the first day you assume your new duties. You'll have to administer the company's program for the prospective retiree. Some companies don't have such a program. In that case your role becomes even more significant.

Many organizations provide graduated time off, over the last few working years, to help the employee get used to the idea of not coming into the office. This may create some work scheduling problems for you as a manager. You can't replace the prospective retiree prematurely, because you want that person to feel needed right up to the day of departure. On the other hand, you can't completely ignore the staffing problems created by the employee's more frequent absences. Some kind of temporary arrangement is best, even if it means using some part-time help. You should not expect your existing staff to pick up the slack unless it can be conveniently handled through duty reassignments.

I know of one situation where a retiring employee—a woman—was told by her male supervisor that she could have virtually unlimited vacation time during her last year on the job. All she had to do was let the supervisor know well in advance when she was going to be gone. This was done. But because he hadn't planned for it, the supervisor had a workload problem. He reacted by getting miffed at the retiring employee every time she talked about exercising the company policy and taking time off. As a result, she stopped taking the time off. He solved his staffing problem, but he failed as an executive in his responsibility to help this woman prepare for her retirement in the way she had wanted to. That's a rotten solution to a staffing problem. In addition, that employee's recollection of the company is colored by that last year on the job during which she could not avail herself of what was a stated company policy.

The Company Program

Many companies prepare their employees for retirement through an official company program that's usually administered by the personnel department. In addition to time off,

109

such a program may include individual counseling, discussion of Social Security benefits and Medicare, hobby and craft demonstrations, exploration of the availability of community programs with members of those agencies invited to lead discussions and to answer questions, seminars with trained professionals about the psychology of preparing for retirement, discussions on budget preparation and adjustment to retirement, information about income-tax implications for retired people with individual consultation, and any other service that a company may consider appropriate for helping their people prepare for this major change in their lifestyle.

If your company does have such a program, you're part of an enlightened organization and your involvement in the process will be primarily supportive. But if your company has no program, or one that isn't very comprehensive, then your own involvement should become heavier.

However, many people who are getting close to retirement look forward to it as the opportunity to do many of the things they haven't had time to do thus far in their lives—these people usually do a good job of preparing themselves for it. They won't be much of a problem for you; your involvement with them will not be difficult. It will again be primarily a supportive role.

Mandatory Retirement

The employee who is tough to work with is one who doesn't want to retire, who dreads the terrible day. Such people often see themselves as being rewarded for 30 years of faithful service by being "put out to pasture." They'll probably use you to see if it's possible to modify the company policy so they can work beyond the retirement age. Some of them will clearly be persons who should not retire. Work is their life. You can help such people by listening to them and making suggestions on where they might find part-time work after retirement. You might be able to work through your personnel department to help them find such an opportunity.

For some of these anxious people, the most valuable service you can provide is your sympathetic attention. They need to talk about their feelings, because in that talk they're trying to adjust to the inevitable, in spite of how much they dislike the idea.

There's a great deal of controversy about mandatory retirement age. Some of the arguments in favor of it are compelling. Everyone in the organization is treated the same and everyone knows when everyone else is going to retire. Such a policy gives younger people in the organization opportunities for promotion. You can plan the training and development of your people on a much more orderly basis if you know exactly when some of them will be retiring. You don't have to make judgments about the continued competency of people who work to more advanced ages.

One strong argument against a mandatory retirement age is that people with valuable experience are lost to the company. Many older employees are alert, in satisfactory physical condition, and able to work additional years. Some employees also consider it a form of discrimination, especially if they want to continue working. Retirement, they argue, should be based on competency. Persons who are able to get the job done should be allowed to work as long as they want to.

My concern is with the personal damage done to the elderly employees who believe they're still making a contribution to the organization whereas management knows their work has deteriorated to the point that makes their retirement necessary. This doesn't happen when everyone retires at the same time.

The policies I particularly object to are those that require all employees to go out at some age but allow the chief executive officer and other privileged executives to stay on beyond that age. In my opinion, such discrimination is unforgivable. I suspect it's a supreme ego trip for executives convinced of their own indispensability.

Your Own Role

As the employee gets closer to retirement, you should indicate that you're available for consultations about the event. You show your interest by calling the employee into your office and asking how his or her retirement plans are coming along. Some executives tell employees, "You know my door is always open. If you're having any problems, be sure to come in." Most employees will not respond to that kind of invitation. Rather, they'll view it as a polite brushoff. Unless they have a serious problem to talk over with you, there's a good chance they won't come in.

You must take the initiative yourself. Your interest in listening to their plans for the future and learning about their misgivings as they move into this new phase of their life could be very helpful to your subordinates. Don't deny them that benefit.

Preparing and improving yourself

(14)

"How am I doing?"

My comments to this point should have convinced you that I believe you have a fairly high opinion of your own capacities and that it's not an unduly inflated viewpoint.

It seems to me that people get awfully mixed up in dealing with this ego thing. There are always those around who want you to feel guilty if you have a high opinion of yourself. Rather, I say, "Love your neighbor as yourself." This implies that your capacity to love your neighbor is determined by your capacity to love yourself. I think the principle applies in management too.

Your Self-Image

Many excellent books have been written on the problem of self-image, and they have important concepts in them for the manager. Perhaps I can share a few basics that I believe will help you in your managerial career.

Most of us live either above or below our self-image. If we have a low opinion of ourself and believe we're going to fail, our subconscious will try to deliver that result to us. Conversely, if we have a high opinion of ourself and think we're going to succeed, our chances for success are greatly increased. I realize that's an oversimplification, but it conveys the thought. If you think success, if you look successful, if you're confident of being successful, you greatly increase your chances to be successful. It's primarily a matter of attitude. If you believe you're a failure, that's what you're likely to be.

To reinforce a successful attitude you need some success along the way. Now that you've moved into your first managerial position every success you have will serve as a building block to further achievements.

It should be obvious that you can't substitute feelings of success for actual accomplishments. You can't have the appearance without any substance. That would be a sham. You'll soon be found out, and to your own disadvantage.

An Impression of Arrogance

One of the most serious problems that I've observed in newly appointed young managers is the impression they give of arrogance. Be careful that you don't handle your feeling of success so that it's misconstrued as arrogance. A manager can feel pride in having been elevated into the managerial ranks without appearing cocky and arrogant. Rather, the impression should be given of *quiet confidence.*

Do you suspect there are people in your organization who don't believe you were the right selection and who'd delight in your failure? That's not only possible, it's quite likely. An appearance that can be construed as arrogance is going to convince these people that they're correct in their assessment of you.

Handling Mistakes

In carrying out your duties as a manager you'll occasionally make mistakes. You'll exercise bad judgment. This happens to all of us. How you view these mistakes is important
in your own development. Be completely honest with yourself and everyone you associate with. Don't try to cover up a
mistake, rationalize it, or, what is even worse, blame it on a
subordinate. New executives have difficulty accepting responsibility for the mistakes of subordinates. Here again is
the "octopus manager" whom we discussed in an earlier
chapter. So skittish are such managers about mistakes that
they decide to avoid criticism by handling all the more complex work themselves. When you do this you shut off your
promotion possibilities and you may even kill yourself with
overwork. A frightening prospect!

So it's difficult for many young leaders to learn to accept
responsibility for the mistakes of subordinates. It's a matter
of self-image. The way to solve the problem is part of your
entire managerial role. You solve it by being a better trainer,
by being a better selector of people, by developing better
internal controls that minimize the mistakes and their impact. The way you view your department and your staff will
have a great influence on how you view yourself.

Self-Infatuation and Self-Contradiction

You have to put forth your best image, but don't be so
successful at it that, like the movie star, you fall for your
own publicity. Be willing to admit to yourself what your
shortcomings are. You'd be surprised at how many executives can't do that. They of course have shortcomings. They
can't be experts at everything. But in ascending to their exalted position, they find that everyone starts catering to
them. It takes an unusual executive to realize that all that
honorific treatment doesn't increase one's intelligence or

117

knowledge. It's easy and pleasant to sit back and accept all that bowing and scraping. The executive is soon convinced that the adoration is deserved. Perhaps the charisma you think is personal is created by the position you hold.

This situation becomes most noticeable in the case of the chief executive officer. Between the beginning manager and the top post are varying degrees of the infallibility syndrome that seems to go with the job. You have to keep an honest perspective of who you are. If tomorrow you were named CEO that wouldn't automatically make you smarter than you were yesterday, but people start listening to you as though you're one of the Three Wise Men. You didn't get smarter, you just have more power. Don't confuse the two!

Pay little attention to what executives say in this regard. Pay more attention to what they do. If an executive says, "I hire people who are smarter than me," what do the words mean? If the executive says, "I encourage my people to disagree with me; I don't want to be surrounded by a bunch of yes men," remember what happened last week when the executive snapped off the head of a subordinate who disagreed. The words are contradicted by the actions.

Throughout your business life you'll encounter executives who espouse beautiful management philosophies. The only problem is that they wield their authority using other philosophies. So be honest with yourself; recognize what you are and try to get your "management talk" reasonably close to your "management performance."

Shortcomings and Prejudices

I don't mean you should advertise your weaknesses. But be willing to admit them to yourself, and do all you can to shore them up. For example, I've always found that the things I don't do well are also the things I don't much like doing either. That can hardly be a coincidence. But you'll get through those chores you don't like if you'll do them early when you're at the height of your energy levels. Every job has aspects to it that you're not going to like; get them done and out of the way so you can do the parts of the job that are the most challenging, the most creative, and the most fun.

Some people like the routine and repetitive parts of the job best. If that's the way you are, then I question whether you should be moving into management and aspiring to even greater responsibilities. It's rarely a problem, because people who like routine tasks seldom move into management. When they do, it's usually a minidisaster.

In addition to recognizing your shortcomings as they apply to your job, be willing to admit attitudes of yours that may be a problem. For example, I'm prejudiced against second-generation wealth. I'm perfectly convinced that people with inherited wealth would fail if they had to start from the bottom like the rest of us. I have to work really hard at overcoming my prejudice when I deal with these people and am forced to view them as equals. My prejudice tells me they're not equals—they're inferior. Conversely, I'm biased in favor of people like myself, who came from a poverty background and worked their way up.

Objectivity

Another aspect of one's self-image is one's ability to be objective. Through the years I've known a great many managers who tell you they're looking at the problem objectively and then proceed to explain their attitudes or solutions in an almost entirely subjective way. When a manager starts off by claiming to be completely objective, ask yourself why the statement was made. Usually, it's an attempt not only at deception but at self-deception. Executives make subjective decisions and then "cover their trail" by telling everyone how objective they were about it. I don't know of anyone who can be completely objective. I have found, however,

119

that the higher the position, the greater the likelihood that subjectivity will be called objectivity.

I bring up this matter because it will help you to analyze how you yourself should view the problem as a manager. "What attitudes, prejudices, or experiences do I have that might cause me to be unnecessarily subjective? How can I approach this problem to discount these subjective considerations, granting that I can't completely purge myself of them? Is my decision fair? Can I defend the decision if I have to?" If you're satisfied with your answers to those questions, then don't agonize over your decisions. And once they're made, don't second-guess yourself, because the vast majority of the decisions will be correct.

Quiet Confidence

Develop quiet confidence about your decision-making ability. As you make more and more decisions, you get better at it. Decisions don't require Solomon-like wisdom; they require the ability to develop the facts. The critical point is to know when you have enough information to make the decision. Generally speaking, if you can get 70 to 80 percent of the information you need, you can make the decision. The inordinate amount of time you'd spend getting the rest of the information would in all probability not result in a different decision anyway. The delay in making the decision is usually more costly than the risk of making a decision based on insufficient information.

The impulsive decision maker leans the other way and makes decisions before an adequate amount of information is obtained. Young managers sometimes believe they have to be fast decision makers and so make decisions too quickly. It will take experience to get the feel as to when you have adequate information to make the decision.

View yourself as a person who isn't afraid to make decisions, but who's also constantly learning the process. This is an area where you need to strike a balance. You don't want to shoot from the hip in making decisions, but you don't want to go to the opposite extreme and never get your gun out of the holster either. Finding that balance will be a learning process. Eventually you'll get to the point where you'll instinctively know when the decision can and should be made.

In summary, view yourself as honestly as you can. Don't be the kind of person who finds reasons for decisions after they've been made. Don't make emotional judgments and rationalize them afterward. When you do that you'll find yourself defending decisions you wish you hadn't made. All of us delude ourselves to some extent, but we help ourselves by holding it down to a bare minimum.

Promotion and Self-Promotion

As mentioned in an earlier chapter, you're judged by the performance of your division, department, or other applicable organizational unit; the people who report to you are therefore more important to your future than the people you report to. That leads directly to the matter of office politics, which comes into play more in the process of scratching your way up the organizational ladder than in any other situation.

Office Politics: Playing the Game

I know of people who are considered "cold turkeys" by those who report to them, but as "warm, generous human beings" by their superiors. Such people are really playing the game, but in the long run they're sure to fail. However much they may succeed in fulfilling their ambitions at their office, they'll fail as human beings.

If getting promoted is more important to you than your

integrity, than being your own person, then I would recommend that you skip the rest of this chapter because you won't like much of what is said in it.

I maintain that almost anyone can succeed temporarily by being a prostitute, but consider the price that's been paid in getting there. Granted that many of the decisions made about promotions will not seem fair to you, and that they won't all be made on the basis of ability. No one guaranteed you that life would be fair, so don't expect it.

I'm not saying that most promotions are made on the basis of something other than fairness and ability. But even though most companies do try to make these decisions fairly, it doesn't always come off that way. Besides, a decision that seems perfectly rational to the executive making it may not seem rational to you, especially if you thought you were the likely candidate for the promotion.

In spite of that, to get promoted you still have to prepare yourself for it. If you depend on luck or serendipity, your chances are greatly diminished. You have everything to gain and nothing to lose by being prepared. Who knows, your opportunity for promotion may come from outside your company. You want to be prepared for that possibility too.

Preparing Your Understudy

As soon as you've mastered your job, you must start looking for an understudy. The reasons for this are obvious. If the company refuses to consider obvious candidates to replace you, it may view you as indispensable in your current position and you may be passed up for promotion.

Finding the appropriate understudy can be a delicate matter. You should not select your crown prince or princess too early. If the candidate doesn't develop properly and fails to demonstrate the skills needed to move into your job, you could have a serious problem at hand. Changing your mind

about a successor you've already selected is like opening a
can of worms.

How you go about preparing for your own replacement is
of critical importance. If you already have an assistant who's
perfectly capable in the job, then it's a matter of helping that
assistant develop as thoroughly and as rapidly as possible.

Give your assistant bits and pieces of your job to perform.
Under no circumstance should you delegate your entire job
to your assistant and then sit back and read newspapers and
business magazines. The company obviously didn't put you
in the position for that purpose.

Allow your assistant to do more and more aspects of your
job until most of it has been learned. Make sure the assistant
does each section of the job frequently enough that it won't
be forgotten. Occasionally, invite the assistant to participate
in the interviewing process when you're hiring new
employees.

Assuming the assistant is performing satisfactorily, start
your political campaign for your prospective replacement.
Make sure your boss knows how well the man or woman is
developing. On performance appraisals, use such terms as
"promotable" and "is developing into an outstanding management prospect." Of course, never say these things if
they're untrue; that would probably work to the disadvantage both of you and of your assistant. But if the assistant is
developing well, communicate it up to the next level without being blatant about it.

You run the risk that the assistant might get promoted out
from under you. It's of course a risk worth taking. Even if
this happens to you several times, you'll get the reputation
of being an outstanding developer of people. That will add
to your own promotability. Besides, you'll find that developing subordinates can be a very highly satisfying experience.
And while you're worrying about preparing your people for

promotion, it's hoped that your own boss is just as concerned about you and your future.

Multiple Choice

If you don't have a single assistant already in place, you should assign parts of your job to several people and see how they run with the added responsibility and the new opportunity. This is indeed to your advantage, since training several replacements at once makes it unlikely that all the candidates will get promoted out from under you. This backstopping in depth will serve you well in emergencies.

Don't be in too big a hurry to move a single candidate into the position of assistant. The moment you name a person as your assistant, the others stop striving for it. That's the trouble with any promotion. Those who don't get it stop aspiring to it, and that usually has an adverse effect on their performance, even though it may be temporary.

Here's a management concept that may be of value to you: Always hold something out for your subordinates to aspire to. If you get to the point where you have to select a single subordinate as your heir apparent, then let the losing candidates know that opportunities still exist for them in other departments, and that you'll help them toward their goal of a promotion.

But as long as you continue to have several prospects vying for the position, you must treat them as equals. Rotate the assignments among them. Make sure that all of them get exposed to all aspects of your job. If you're gone from the office occasionally, put each in charge of the operation in turn. Give them all a chance at managing the personnel aspects of the job too.

On some regular basis, meet with all the candidates at once and discuss your job with them. Don't say, "Let's discuss my job"; rather, talk about some specific problems they've encountered. All of them will benefit from the discussion. If one of them had to face an unusual management problem in your absence, why shouldn't all of them benefit from the experience?

The Perils of Indispensability

Again let me point out the importance of not allowing yourself to become indispensable. Some executives trap themselves into this kind of situation. In their effort to ensure the quality of the work, they request that all difficult questions be referred to them. It doesn't take long for employees to figure out that anything out of the ordinary will soon be going to you as the boss. It isn't the time taken from your day that creates problems. The more fundamental trouble is that your people soon stop trying to work out the more complex problems by themselves.

I believe it's important that your people be encouraged to find answers on their own. They'll be better employees for it. There are limits, of course, to the areas of responsibility that can be delegated to them, but I've always felt that you're better off erring on the side of too much latitude in delegating responsibility than too little. I think it takes a better manager to allow staff members some responsibility while still assuring them that the executive is accountable for their performance.

I'm sure you've heard people worrying about whether the company would get along without them while they're on vacation. They have it backward: their real worry is that the company *will* get along just fine without them. The executive who's doing the right kind of job in developing employees and backup management can leave with the assurance that the department will function very smoothly in his or her absence. The truly efficient and dedicated executive, indeed, has progressed to the point where he or she can even be gone permanently—to a promotion in another company. I've known managers who, in a misguided view of what their job

125

required, made themselves indispensable and spent the rest of their business careers proving it—by never being moved from that position.

The main problem with such people is that they don't understand what the job of management is about. Management isn't doing—it's seeing that it's done.

The Lazy Employee

Another practice I'd like to recommend is that of indulging the lazy employee. Before you think I've completely lost my mind, let me explain. A lot of lazy employees I've known are ceaselessly on the lookout for easier ways to do things. Employees who enjoy all the detail and all of the busywork are not going to figure out ways to eliminate it—because that's their thing. Not so with the lazy employee, who'll work hard and long at finding an easier way to do it.

If you provide me with industrious people who like fussing endlessly over minute trivia, I'll never be able to reduce staff. However, sprinkle my staff with a few lazy souls and eventually I'll be able to reduce the number of employees. As some people leave, I won't have to replace them. And I know well that the line going straight to upper management's heart is "reduce staff and cost."

Your Predecessor

It helps a great deal if your predecessor in the job was a real dunderhead who left the place in a shambles. Unless you're a complete idiot, you'll look like a champion in comparison. That's preferable to stepping into a smooth-running operation. What you can do with statistics alone is amazing. So if you ever have a choice between moving into an area that appears to be in chaos and moving into a nice clean operation, go into the chaos every time. You'll never regret it.

Continuing Your Education

Something else you should consider in preparing yourself for promotion is to extend your knowledge about the business you're in. It's not enough to become expert in your restricted area of responsibility. You must understand more about your company's entire operation.

You can acquire this additional knowledge in several ways. There's hardly a business firm in the country today that doesn't stock many books in its library about that kind of endeavor. You can broaden your knowledge through selected readings. Your own boss may be able to recommend published material that fits closely into your own company's operation and philosophy. No boss is ever insulted when asked for advice. However, a word of caution: Don't ask for advice too often, because your boss will either suspect you can't make up your own mind about too many things or figure you're seeking a favor. Neither of these reactions will help your cause.

If your company offers education programs, sign up for them. Even if you can't see gaining any immediate benefit from them, they'll serve you well over the long haul. In addition, you're displaying an eagerness to learn.

Tooting Your Own Horn—But Softly

A point about playing personal politics is in order here. You can be the greatest thing since graham crackers, but if you're the only one who knows it you won't go anywhere with your many talents. So not only should you make sure your achievements are known to your superiors, but how you go about spreading the glad tidings is also crucial. If you're obviously tooting your own horn, people are going to react negatively to it. You must be subtle. Keep in mind that no one's interest in your promotability coincides with your own.

For example, let's say the local community college is offering courses that you think would be helpful to you in your job and in making you more promotable. You might sign up for such a course and complete it satisfactorily, yet no one in your organization would ever know about it. Let's assume the course you're taking is in accounting. Here are some ways to make sure your boss and the company know you're taking the course:

—Send a note to the personnel department—and a carbon copy to your boss—asking that your personnel records show you're taking the course. This puts it in your personnel file where anyone examining your record and considering you for promotion will see it. On completing the course, again notify the personnel department of the achievement.

—Use the casual conversation approach with your boss. "One of the fellas in my accounting class said something funny last night. . . ." The boss will ask, "What accounting class?"

—Place books on your desk that will prompt the desired question.

—Ask your boss for clarification of a class discussion item that you didn't fully understand.

—Invite a classmate to the office to have lunch with you and introduce her to your boss: "Mr. Smith, I'd like you to meet my accounting course classmate, Nelda Jones."

I'm sure you get the idea. The more subtle you become in your self-advertisement, the less likely that it will appear as horn-tooting.

With an apology to the King James Version, "What profit it a man if he becometh the most qualified employee in the company and no one else knoweth it?" You must develop techniques along this line because too few bosses will approach you and say, "Tell me, what are you doing to prepare yourself for promotion?"

The reader may react negatively when I talk about being political. The word connotes making backroom deals and compromising one's principles in order to get ahead. That kind of politics does of course exist in an office too. Some of it can be funny and some of it can be very vicious. But in speaking of preparing yourself for promotion, I'm using the word political in its finest sense. I mean making sure your superior characteristics and accomplishments are known to those who make the promotion decisions. I refer to it as being political in a positive way; you could just as easily refer to it as common-sense communication.

Some executives blithely announce that if you do your job to the best of your ability, the promotions and raises will take care of themselves. But if they don't know what you're doing, how can they take your accomplishments into consideration in making their promotion decision? You'll often hear executives mouthing clichés that they think are great pearls of wisdom. At least two things may be wrong about some of the clichés: the executive making them doesn't manage that way, and the statement is no longer true. The bit about the raises and the promotions taking care of themselves applies here.

You must develop your own style of communicating the important aspects of your development in the company, but you must see to it that the way you get the message across doesn't offend others or make you appear pushy.

But Is the Game Worth the Candle?

Working toward a promotion is an almost constant state of mind—unless, of course, you're the kind of person who reaches a certain point and then loses interest in moving further. There's surely nothing wrong with the attitude, "I don't want to pay the price of moving to the next rung of the ladder." That's indeed healthier than finding out too late that your assumption that you're still promotable is not shared by management.

Unfortunately, in too many cases, you're never told, so you keep on busting your butt to be promoted and don't know that your chances are nil. One reason, I suspect, is that your superiors know how valuable you are in the present job and they don't want to lose you, even though they feel you've topped out. Sometimes the awful reality doesn't dawn on you until you're almost at the age when another promotion is unlikely.

You have a right to know where you stand in the company, and I see absolutely nothing wrong with pressing for the information before it's too late. If you think top management is wrong in judging you nonpromotable, there are things you can do about it. One way is to seek additional challenge by changing jobs; another is to supplement your job with new, additional challenges—hobbies and social or civic activities—that will make your life more interesting and rewarding.

A word of caution: Don't spend a lot of time worrying about promotion until you have a solid handle on your current job. Mastery of that job is your first priority. Only then should you start your campaign to get promoted. It really is a campaign, although primarily a one-person effort. Others with nearly as much interest in your getting promoted are subordinates who believe they have a shot at your position once you've moved up.

Don't start making noises about promotability too soon. Your boss may consider it premature. You've finally got things in your area going smoothly; the boss can now relax a bit—the company's investment in you is paying off. However, if all of a sudden you start talking about moving on to something better, the boss will consider you an impatient ingrate. Promotion, of course, often crosses your mind, but some things are best kept to yourself for a while.

You may have a master plan. You may have a particular ultimate goal in mind. It may even be the chief executive officer's position. But you must proceed by aiming your sights on interim goals. You must perform each of the assignments in super fashion if you're to move on to your next goal. Each of the stops along the way to your final goal becomes critically important. Each offers a reassessment opportunity. At each step you must determine whether you're willing to pay the price required to get you to the next step. There's nothing wrong with deciding the price is too high and that you don't want to pay it.

I've observed, however, that not every step up the ladder requires that you pay a higher price. Sometimes that's just propaganda put out by people in higher positions to prove to everyone else that they deserve to be there. So in making your way to the next position up the ladder toward your goal, be prepared for dense diversionary smoke screens. And assuming it does require paying an additional price, weigh that price against the reward the higher position promises. Is the game worth the candle?

The Executive Whose Job You Want

In analyzing the situation accurately, you'll often find that the person holding the position you aspire to is a workaholic —and by choice. Many of the tasks the workaholic performs are occupational hobbies, indulged in compulsively—every weekend and every night. Sometimes these people are escaping from pressures at home, even though they'd be the last to admit it. Working at the office is a socially acceptable way of staying away from home. But just because a situation exists doesn't mean it has to be that way. Sometimes your workaholic boss is poor at delegating authority and thus cannot significantly decrease the burdens of the position.

Obviously it's not up to you to tell your superior he or she appears to be working harder than the job actually requires. At this point let's admit that all of us to some extent attempt to make ourselves and our job look a bit more important or a bit tougher than it really is. We all want to be cast in as favorable a light as possible.

Seeking Advice

The one person who can realistically view the job you aspire to is the predecessor of the incumbent. That person has the distance and disinterest to give you candid answers to your questions. That person also will outrank you by at least two levels on the organization chart and in all likelihood will be older than you. How you approach this executive will largely determine the kind of response you'll get. Again, don't make the approach too quickly if you're still fairly new in your current position.

However, let's assume that a respectable length of time has passed and you've decided you're going to approach Mr. Hunter. You don't approach him at all if he stands directly in the chain of command as it affects you personally. That is, if Mrs. Rogers holds the job you aspire to, and if she reports directly to Mr. Hunter and you report directly to her, under no circumstances do you go around her to talk to Mr. Hunter about the job she holds. I'm assuming here that Mrs. Rogers does not report to Mr. Hunter. It's even better if Mrs. Rogers is not your boss. You have to sort out these lines of reporting in your own company and make the decision on whether or not to talk to Mr. Hunter. I'm assuming you exercise sound judgment in thse matters. In any case, the decision is made: you're going to talk to Mr. Hunter. How do you approach him and what do you say to set the stage properly?

As mentioned earlier, most managers or executives are flattered when asked for advice. Your opening might go something like this:

"Mr. Hunter, I'd like to get the benefit of your experience. In looking around at positions in the company that I think I'd like to aspire to, I've found that the job Mrs. Rogers holds might be a challenging one. I know you held that position at one time. Did you find it a challenging and interesting aspect of your career? Do you think it's reasonable for me to aspire to that job?"

You may not be able to get it all out as a nonstop monologue, but at least you've put the matter on the agenda. You then sit back, remain silent, and let Mr. Hunter lay his wisdom on you.

Let's analyze the recommended opening gambit. First of all, you've asked your superior for the benefit of his experience. You've thereby put him in a generous frame of mind. Second, you've stated that you've been looking around at positions in the company that you might aspire to. This indicates that your horizons are broad; you haven't limited your search to the area you're currently working in. Third, you didn't say to Mr. Hunter that the job Mrs. Rogers holds *is* a challenging position; you said it *might be* a challenging one. You're going to let Mr. Hunter tell *you* about the challenge in the job. After all, you want the benefit of his experience.

You then asked him if he found the job interesting. If he had found it to be a dull, methodical job that bored the hell out of him, that's information you ought to have. From there you went on to ask him if he thought it was reasonable for you to aspire to the job. How he answers that question will depend on how well he knows you and the kind of performer you are in your current position.

You might also go directly to Mrs. Rogers. As in the preceding example, this depends on several factors, including where you and Mrs. Rogers are relative to each other on the organization chart. Here again your judgment will have to prevail. But sometimes the direct approach is bold enough to be quite effective.

"Mrs. Rogers, I wonder if I could ask your advice on a matter of my own personal development. I know the company always has its eye out for people who are promotable, and I'm positive that if there's a list of promotable people you're on it. I'm interested in having a shot at your job when you're promoted. I'd like to find out your feelings about your job and also whether you think it's reasonable for me to aspire to it."

Again, you may not be able to deliver the monologue eloquently, without stumbling but it's the kind of language you want to start with.

In this opener with Mrs. Rogers, you're asking for advice. You can expect a favorable response. Second, you've told her you think she's going somewhere in the organization. She certainly won't find that offensive. Third, you didn't say you wanted her job when she was promoted. You merely said you wanted a shot at it—a fair chance. Who could object to that? You then asked if she thought it was reasonable for you to aspire to the job. As one of my attorney friends says, you knew the answer before you asked the question.

Both the conversation with Mr. Hunter and the one with Mrs. Rogers require the use of finesse, or, in the vernacular of the street, *moxie.*

Acquiring a Sponsor

One favorable side effect of such a conversation is the acquisition of a *sponsor.* It can't hurt to have executive power on your side. In fact, being sponsored by a couple of people higher in the organization who are stars themselves is a great thing to have going for you.

Most sponsors are acquired by careful cultivation. Few

sponsors get the idea on their own. Something had to happen to give them the thought; usually it was a favorable impression you created one way or another.

Style and Merit

Achieving the objectives discussed in this chapter requires satisfactory performance on your part, and confidence in yourself. Oftentimes, the difference between a satisfactory and a great job is image or style. I believe your style colors a superior's perception of your performance, especially if the style is one your superior reacts positively to. But a bad or offensive style is similarly critical in evoking a negative response.

There's a vast difference between doing a great job and maximizing the mileage you get out of that, on the one hand, and conning people into thinking you're doing an outstanding job when you're not cutting the mustard, on the other. I'm assuming you're capable, you're making your way up the organization ladder on your merits.

15

Organizing your own time

Have you ever gone home from the office with the feeling, "I didn't accomplish any of the things I wanted to get done today"? We all have days like that, spent entirely in putting out brushfires. Sometimes that can't be helped, but if it's happening to you regularly, part of the problem may be your own lack of organization.

My Own Approach

My own approach toward this book is a good example. Almost every day I'd set a goal of writing a full chapter, yet an entire week would sometimes go by without my having written a single line. The reason was the compulsion I felt to block out several solid hours so I could tackle a chapter. The system got me nowhere. Then I decided that my effort had to be broken up into smaller pieces. So my goal became to write two handwritten pages each day. Occasionally I'd miss a day; I then set a goal of four pages for the next day.

As a result of the change in emphasis, I started getting material written, even though the demands on my time from other responsibilities had not changed. The only change was my attitude toward and approach to the problem. One evening I sat down to write my two pages—and ended up writing a dozen. If I had established a goal for that day of twelve pages, because of the lateness of the hour I wouldn't even have begun to write that evening.

The List

A number of years ago I read an article about the late American industrialist Henry Kaiser. As you know, Henry Kaiser accomplished a great deal in his life, including the establishment of a company that built cargo vessels called Liberty ships during World War II. The ships were completely constructed in a matter of days, truly a spectacular accomplishment.

The first thing Kaiser did on entering the office in the morning was to sit at his desk with a legal-size pad on which he listed the items he wished to accomplish that day. I don't recall that he attempted to list them in a priority order. During the day, the list remained on top of the desk. As a goal was accomplished, a line was drawn through it on the pad. Goals that didn't get lined out that day would be put on the next day's list.

I tried this simple approach to organizing my day and was pleasantly surprised at how much more I started to accomplish. You're forced to plan the day's activities as you write the day's objectives on the pad. That's probably the greatest value of the technique.

There are several different approaches that can be used in planning your day. Some managers believe they ought to list the objectives in the order of their importance and complete them in that sequence. Others prefer making three lists. The first contains emergency matters that are bleeding for attention. The second comprises items that are not emergency in nature but have to be done. The third includes things that can be done when you have the time. This is a fine arrangement if your day is so highly controlled that you need not worry about being deterred from making your appointed rounds by unexpected circumstances.

Such a regimented day has never been possible for me. I can't control the interruptions. I can't shut off the telephone. So I just make my little daily list of every variety of objective, from dealing with emergencies to planning long-range projects that I'm hoping to get around to some day. Included are matters that are putting no pressure on me at the moment.

Another reason for not breaking my list down into categories is my knowledge of what has to be done immediately and what can wait. Let's face it, I know I can't survive as a manager if I ignore my emergencies. So even if the emergency is number twenty on my list, I'm not going to take care of nineteen other tasks ahead of the panic item.

Anyone else looking at my list would probably think I had lost my mind, because I write objectives down as they enter my head without worrying about any order or priority for accomplishing them. I'll even put personal items on the list, like reminding myself that I'm supposed to stop at the grocery store for a loaf of bread on my way home. A long-range project may appear on my list every day for a couple of months. Eventually, I'll get tired of repeatedly listing it and I'll get it done. I start feeling like a procrastinator if I keep it on my list too long.

One also gets a psychological lift out of drawing a line through tasks that have been completed. It's great to sit there late in the afternoon reflecting on the day's activities and see that the majority of the items on your list have been lined out.

Don't throw the list away when you leave the office. The next morning, yesterday's list will serve two purposes. It will remind you of all you accomplished the day before— there's nothing wrong with that—and will inform you of what remained unaccomplished. These latter items then go on the new list. That's especially important for long-range projects that might get accidentally dropped from the list. Too many creative ideas and projects get away from us because we didn't write them down.

I once read that the late Duke Ellington kept paper and pencil on his night table for use in jotting down musical ideas that would come to him in bed at night. I'm sure you've had the experience I've often had: a great thought comes to you during the night, but in the morning it's gone. No matter how you strain to recapture it, it eludes you and you can't bring it back.

Homework

Nowadays—at least in my part of the country—nearly every male executive (junior and senior) carries an attaché case to and from the office. I believe the attaché case serves primarily as a purse. I'll admit right here that I carry an attaché case back and forth between my home and the office, even though I seldom take any work with me. If I have unfinished work that can't wait, I'll go back to the office in the evening or on Saturday. That's easy for me here in Lincoln, Nebraska; I can get to the office by car in ten minutes. For a suburbanite commuting to an office in one of the nation's big cities, it may be more practical to take work home occasionally. However, you should not be taking routine work home on a regular basis; that would indicate you're not very well organized. Taking creative work home makes sense, however.

My attaché case contains things I want with me whether I'm at the office or at home. So, from that point of view, it serves for me the purpose that a purse serves for a woman.

My Day at the Office

In preparing your daily list, you have to decide what will be done in what order. As mentioned earlier, you'll almost certainly take care of the emergencies first. You'll then glance over the list and decide what to do next. My own usual procedure is to do things I don't like and get them out of the way, thus freeing myself to do what I enjoy. I often move very early to a task I can complete quickly, thereby setting myself up mentally in an accomplishing spirit. Even though I know full well that I'm psyching myself, it still works.

Every once in a while I'll arrive at the office, all hell will immediately break loose, and I won't get my list made. Riding home in my car, I may have the uncomfortable feeling that I didn't accomplish a great deal that day. That kind of thing happened more earlier in my career, before making my list had become a habit. It's now a rare day indeed that my list doesn't get made.

The Weekend List

My wife was a list maker for me long before I read about Henry Kaiser's approach. She makes lists of things she wants me to do around the house on weekends. Fortunately, that doesn't happen every weekend. However, I've become so habitual a list maker that I now make the weekend house-chores list myself. I don't necessarily transfer uncompleted chores to next weekend's list—there's no sense in carrying this passion for order and efficiency too far.

The Closed Period

Some organizations follow a procedure you may want to use in mapping out your own day to accomplish more. An office will have what I call a "two-hour closed period." The office does its business as usual, except that no one in the office goes to see anyone else—no one makes intra-office phone calls and no company meetings are ever scheduled during this closed period. Genuine emergencies are handled expeditiously; calls from clients or customers or outside phone calls are accepted.

The idea has a great deal of merit. It means you'll have two hours each day when no one from within the company is going to call you on the phone or come into your office. It gives you an opportunity to control what you do during the specified period. Perhaps some person got the idea while working in the office on a weekend and noticing how much more was accomplished then than in the same period of time during the week. But the idea is feasible only if you don't shut off your customers or clients during the closed period. It's an idea an entire organization can use to advantage.

Remembering and Reflecting

Here's a bit of advice that won't do a whole lot for you at the office but will help you remember things you're supposed to stop for on the way home. Put a reminder in the pocket where you keep your car keys. Then, on your way to the parking lot at the end of the workday, you'll reach into your pocket for the car keys and *presto!*—there it is. Maybe you don't get distracted from doing personal errands the way I do; you may therefore not need such reminders. I do.

A final suggestion about how best to organize your time.

Plan to have a quiet period each day. You may not get it every day, but it's important that you set aside some time for daydreaming and reflection. It's vital to the inner person. Also, problems that seem insurmountable often ease into proper perspective during these quiet times.

16

Managing, participating in, and leading meetings

In Chapter 15, mention was made of companies that have "closed periods" during which office personnel don't phone one another and don't attend meetings. That gives them a certain amount of uninterruptible time each day. Indeed, I occasionally think the productivity of the entire country would be greatly increased if all office meetings of more than two people, in business and government, were banned for one year.

The Meeting Surrogate

Another suggestion is that each company designate a few people as professional meeting attenders—surrogates for everyone else in the office. One person might be a surrogate for 20 managers and executives. Every time you're summoned to a meeting, you could send your surrogate; then, if anything important happened (which, of course, is highly unlikely), the surrogate could condense it and report it back to you. The only people who would fail to see both the value and the humor in such a proposal are those who like to go to meetings.

People who like to go to meetings are easily identifiable. They're the ones who do most of the talking and wander off the topic as a means of prolonging the meeting. An additional benefit for them in the ploy is that it delays their having to go back to work where their progress might be measured. This type of person should be selected as one of the meeting surrogates.

The idea of the meeting surrogate is so radical and yet so practical that it will not be adopted in our lifetime, so we'd all better face up to the hard reality of having to attend some meetings.

Advance Notice

Another proposal that might be considered bold is to announce the agenda of a meeting in advance. That would give people a chance to prepare somewhat for the meeting. But such a procedure would require a chairperson who has a lot of charity in his or her makeup. Some people chairing a meeting need to feel superior, and they can achieve that goal only if they're the only one who knows what's going to be discussed.

Whenever possible, find out what's going to be considered at the meeting and come prepared. What decisions will be made? What information do I need to vote intelligently on the required decisions? In what way can my particular experiences with the company provide valuable input to the entire committee? What points of view are the other members of the committee likely to bring to the meeting? Is the chairperson's point of view likely to prevail? Do I agree or disagree with it? Do I have a strong opinion on the subject, or do I need a lot more facts? Am I completely neutral on the issue? Are certain people on the committee going to fight for their position or is the entire committee likely to be neutral until the facts come out and the discussion develops?

Mistakes Managers Make

There's one compulsion that many managers too readily give in to at meetings: they feel obligated to say something, assuming that their silence will be interpreted as ignorance. In the words of the old saw, "It's better to remain silent and be thought a fool, than to open your mouth and remove all doubt." Obviously, you can't sit in stony silence throughout the entire meeting, but you shouldn't feel compelled to speak just for the sake of saying something, either.

How you handle yourself in the first few meetings will create the impression that many of the other attendants will carry with them for quite a while. You're much better off choosing your statements at the first few meetings quite carefully. If what you say is well thought out and adds insight leading toward solution of the problem, you'll carry far more weight than if you merely try to be agreeable and utter a lot of insignificant prattle: "I sure agree with that." "That's interesting." "I'm sure most people haven't thought of it that way." "That's right; that's for sure."

Another mistake I've seen new managers make in meetings with other executives is to seize the first opportunity to say something uncomplimentary about a subordinate. This inclines me strongly to the view that such people may not have been ready for management yet. They doubtless expect and possibly even demand loyalty from their own staff; they clearly owe the same loyalty to their subordinates. Loyalty and respect have to move in both directions, or it won't be long before they fail to exist in either direction.

You don't gain anything in the eyes of your peers if you knock one of your subordinates. If you're in a situation where frank assessment of an employee's performance is imperative, then you'll want to be completely honest in your appraisal. But such a remark as "I've got a couple of real deadheads in my department in Louie and Joe" is inappropriate. While the statement doesn't do Louie and Joe any good, it harms the person who makes it most of all.

Keeping Your Cool

One rule to fix firmly in yourself as a behavior pattern is never to lose your cool in a meeting. Unfortunately, every company has executives who use meetings to make provocative statements that are designed to get under the skin of others. Some of them do it unconsciously, never realizing they're creating turmoil. Those who do it deliberately are compulsive mischief makers who like to keep things stirred up. Some of your peers and superiors perhaps enjoy testing you to see what it takes to get you to lose your cool. The ability to hold your own in such situations will stand you in good stead in all aspects of your management career.

One critical test in this area will come the first time someone in a meeting indicates that part or all of a certain problem derives from lack of performance in your department. Your spontaneous reaction might be, "Like hell it is! You're out of your mind!" That's the wrong way to react, even though it's perfectly natural and completely understandable. You'd be much better off responding, "I suppose that's possible. Maybe you know something about my department I don't know. I'd be interested in some facts and figures."

Usually, the more defensive you are when someone makes a statement about your area of responsibility, the more inclined people will be to believe the charge is justified. However, if it doesn't seem to shake you up, if you seem to be completely in control, they'll wonder about the veracity of the statement. If you're sure of what the situation is and you know your adversary is incorrect, you can remain cool because you know what the outcome will be. Any kind of investigation of the facts will support your position. It's more difficult to remain believable and look confident if you lose your cool and become defensive.

Of course, there are people who'll accuse you of being defensive when all you're doing is answering the question. They do it because they know how people hate being called defensive in an office situation. It has the aspects of a self-fulfilling prophecy. You're not being defensive, but when someone accuses you of being defensive you sound defensive while denying it.

I believe your best bet is always to come down on the side of understatement rather than overstatement. If you oversell your point of view, it may come back to haunt you. You're much better off selling your point of view logically, in easily understandable terms. When you sell it emotionally, the support you can receive can float away on another wave of emotion that takes an opposite course. If you can explain your position rationally, and document the case you make for it, that support will not so readily be lost to you.

Not only in meetings but in the entire managerial process, people too often tend to work backward. They make the decision that gratifies them emotionally, and then dig out facts and figures to justify the decision on a logical basis. Don't fool yourself. You'll occasionally make an emotional decision, but don't kid yourself into believing you arrived at it logically. You'll of course make some decisions that are both emotional and logical; the ones that can get you in trouble are those that are emotional and lacking in logic.

All of us make emotional decisions on occasion. Show me an executive who never makes an emotional decision and

I'll show you either a robot or a person who has perfected the process of rationalization to the point of being an exact science.

Yes Men (Male and Female)

Another problem that's characteristic of meetings is the tendency for the yes man (male or female) to surface. This will happen primarily when the meeting includes executives holding various ranks on the organization chart. As a student of human nature, you'll see both subtle and not so subtle forms of obsequiousness on the part of yes men in your organization—perhaps the word *brown-nosing* won't seem out of place to describe such odious behavior.

We must be completely honest with each other. The reason there are yes men is because some people believe it pays off. It doesn't matter to some that the price being paid for advancement is too high. Then there are those who prostitute themselves in a business situation so regularly that they don't even know they're doing it.

This is an area where I must be careful in advising you. My impulses tend to carry me in the opposite direction: even when I agree with the boss, I'm reluctant to show it because I don't like even the appearance of being a yes man. But that extreme is bad too. It's almost reverse snobbery. Ideally, you should openly agree with your boss when you do honestly agree, and disagree when that's what you truly feel. You're in trouble if you have a boss who speaks loudly against being surrounded by a bunch of yes men, but who doesn't take kindly to disagreement. It's not what is said, it's what the action proves.

Frankly, if the company you're with is one that fosters yes-man behavior up and down the organization chart, then I suggest you consider leaving, because there's no way you can survive in a place like that without selling your soul. Some things are more important than getting promoted or receiving a raise—maintaining your integrity, for example. If your integrity can be bought for a promotion or a raise, then you don't have any, baby!—integrity, that is.

It's fairly easy to pick out the yes men (male or female) in a meeting. They're the ones who glance up and down the table to check out the lay of the land before committing themselves. Then, when they do speak, their statements are so tentative or ambiguous that, should a superior start to disagree, they have only to make a slight shift in their position to be completely in accord with the higher authority.

People like that are worthless at a meeting. Unfortunately, some executives like being surrounded by such completely predictable subordinates. They believe what the boss believes. On the other hand, I've seen really sharp executives putting potential yes men through some of the most intricate tap-dancing and side-stepping you can imagine. These executives are so sure of themselves that they'll change their own position 180 degrees during a long meeting just to see how far the yes men will go with them. The terminal cases go with them all the way.

If you're going to make a contribution to a meeting, then you have to be in a secure enough position to say what you think. If that can't occur, there's no sense in being part of that committee.

Refusing to Go Along with the Crowd

When you feel compelled to disagree with other people or with a committee, do it in a diplomatic way. The person you're disagreeing with isn't wrong—it's the position taken by that person that's incorrect. Keep that always in mind and you'll get along much better than if you have people believing you're going after them personally. Unfortunately, you'll find there are people who take any disagreement as personal. That's their particular personality quirk and there's nothing you can do about it, except to make sure in your own mind that it's not personal with you.

Another mistake made by people new to management or committee meetings has to do with their reaction to questions they can't answer. There's a temptation to bluff your way through that kind of situation. You'll usually be found out if you do this too often. It's best to say, "I'm not sure" or "I don't know." If you bluff, you're likely to give a wrong answer and thereby create even more problems.

When you're new in your position, your "I don't know" will be tolerated for a while. However, with time that protective "I don't know" ought to diminish greatly. And it will, as you achieve a better understanding of your job and know what you're doing.

One of my wishes for you is that you don't spend an inordinate amount of time going to a great variety of committee meetings. They cut into your productive time. Most committee meetings don't accomplish much. I often get the feeling that committees were invented as a method of "spreading the blame" for decisions that may be unpopular. I see nothing wrong with asking to be excused from a meeting when you believe you have higher-priority items to work on. You can't do it too often, but once in a while it'll work.

As you approach a meeting, set your emotions at a high frustration level. For example, one great frustration is having to spend a lot of time in a meeting whose purpose seems insignificant compared with the more important things waiting for you in your office. As you "do time" in a corporation, especially if you're in a large office, you'll find many things that frustrate you. If you don't learn to handle these frustrations, you'll get ulcers, high blood pressure, or worse.

With a bit of practice you can learn to be "alone" even in a crowd. You can actually build a psychological protective shield around yourself, so that even if you see the frustration possibilities building up, you've developed a toughness that they bounce harmlessly off of. You're aware of them, but they don't get through to you. It's a kind of toughness that says, "I am the master of my fate: I am the captain of my soul." This ability will be of value beyond your meetings. You decide what filters through to you. You're aware of what's going on, but you decide where you'll allow your emotions to get involved.

Chairing a Committee

In your role as a new manager, the chances are remote that you'll be made chairperson of a permanent committee. However, you may end up as chairperson of a special task force or of a subcommittee. The best training for chairing a committee is participation in committee activities and the ordeal of suffering through meetings that are badly run. If you've never attended a well-run committee meeting, you might not fully appreciate what you're missing. Some managers spend their entire business life without ever having attended a well-run meeting.

You can run a well-organized meeting that gets through its business with dispatch and still be a rotten chairperson. It seems to me that there are two extremes. One is the chairperson who allows the meeting to drift through irrelevant topics for long periods and who generally lacks control. In this case, the meeting takes much too long for the business at hand. The other extreme is the dictatorial chairperson who has so much clout in the organization that no one on the committee can buck him or her. Such people know what they want done, and they tolerate no major disagreement. They get a meeting over with quickly. It may be a rubber-stamp committee, but it's efficient. Obviously, we want to be somewhere between these two extremes.

Certain Basics

There are certain basics you should remember if you're going to be successful at presiding over meetings. The fundamental responsibility of a presiding officer is to conduct the business of the committee with fairness and dispatch, allowing all members an opportunity to participate in the deliberations. Most committees within a company are run informally; you'll seldom chair a committee that requires you to be an expert parliamentarian. (In that event, of course, you'll have to become familiar with those more technical approaches.)

As chairperson, you should see that everyone receives an agenda well in advance of the meeting. This will give members the opportunity to prepare themselves for the questions and issues to be considered. The timing of the agenda depends on the frequency of the meetings. If you meet monthly, distributing the agenda about ten days in advance should be sufficient. If you meet weekly, you can have some mutually agreed upon time for distributing both the minutes of the past meeting and the agenda of the coming meeting.

Distributing the minutes to people before the meeting can be quite a time-saver. Committee members will read the minutes before the next meeting. If you go through the formality of approving the minutes, there'll usually be a motion to approve the minutes as published. The only exception is when a member feels that a correction in the minutes is necessary. These corrections are usually minor.

Another advantage of having an agenda is its disciplinary effect on the entire committee. Members know what their objectives are. You'll usually get no static if you always provide a spot on your agenda for "other business." This gives members an opportunity to discuss whatever other items they think should be discussed by the committee. It also says to committee members, "We'll take up other business after we've disposed of these first priorities."

As chairperson, you should let members know they can request that items be added to the agenda. I favor identifying these requests by the person making them. This saves you time because if other committee members want additional information about the particular agenda item added, say, by Mr. Smith, they'll call Mr. Smith instead of you, the chairperson.

Before the meeting begins, people will usually be carrying on various private conversations. Calling the meeting to order is therefore necessary. It can usually be done by speaking in a louder voice, or tapping a coffee cup with a spoon and saying, "Shall we get started?" If it's a more formal setting, you might say, "Can we come to order, please?"

Keep the committee on the subject. Committees have a way of drifting away from the business at hand. The chairperson must be a diplomat in keeping members attentive to the task in front of them. Your repertoire should include phrases like this:

"That's very interesting, Fred. How does that tie back into our discussion of agenda item number 6?" "I'm afraid we're drifting away from the subject. Even though this is very interesting, we'd better get back to our agenda." "We're beginning to make some of the same arguments for the second and third time. Are we ready to make a decision on this matter?" "I don't want to discourage a complete discussion on this, but the hour is getting late, and we still have much material to cover."

One problem a new manager may encounter is in chairing a committee that consists of some executives in the organization who outrank him or her. Sometimes the manager looks to that ranking executive for major leadership on the committee. If the company had wanted that executive to be the dominant force on the committee, he or she would have been designated as chairperson instead of you.

The most uncomfortable situation for a new manager is when the president sits on the committee. It's difficult to treat that officer like any other member, but I think you have to stay as close to that posture as possible. Obviously, if the president wants to digress from the agenda for any reason, it isn't too smart to say, "Let's get back to the agenda." In most companies, the president won't be the problem. The problem will be other members of the committee who are trying to impress the top executive.

Most organizations are not going to put you in the position of chairing a committee consisting of people who outrank you. You'll usually chair a committee consisting of peers and a few subordinates.

The rules of common sense should prevail in chairing meetings. Keep your cool. Don't let anyone press your panic button. Be courteous to everyone on the committee. Avoid putting anyone down. Always deal with the problem at hand —don't get involved in personalities, no matter how much anyone else does. Be better organized than anyone else on the committee. Develop the kind of trustful relationship with everyone on the committee that will prompt them always to come to you beforehand with unusual items for the group, thereby avoiding unpleasant surprises. Be fair to everyone, even those whose viewpoints you disagree with.

I believe you can do a better job of building this kind of relationship with committee members if as chairperson you vote only to break ties. I know of government committees that require a roll-call vote from everyone including the chairperson. I see no need for this in a business situation. Avoid it.

You can be fair and considerate and still leave no doubt as to who's in charge and running the meeting. If you're fair to all viewpoints, you'll have the respect of the entire committee. At times one or two members will argue a position that the majority becomes impatient with; the fair chairperson will see that minority opinions are heard and will not allow the majority to overwhelm the dissenter. If you handle the controversy properly, you'll get the respect of members of the majority because they know on some other issue they might hold a minority position.

Being a successful committee chairperson is another opportunity to demonstrate the quality of your management skills.

$$\textbf{17}$$

Learning to be an adequate public speaker

I'm repeatedly amazed by the number of capable executives who can't handle a public speaking situation. Standing up there on the platform, they come off as the dullest clod imaginable. The impression the audience gets of them is that they're not very good on the job either.

Prior Preparation

Many managers are rotten public speakers because they wait until they find themselves in a speaking situation before they do anything about it. By then it's too late. You can be the greatest manager in the world and your light will be hidden under a bushel if you don't prepare yourself to be a public speaker.

Because so few people in managerial positions prepare themselves to speak publicly, you'll have a leg up on most of them if you learn how it's done. Public speaking frightens many people, and so they avoid it like the plague. But what they probably don't consider early in their career is that although speeches to outside groups may be avoided, the speech that will take place within their own office must be faced.

It may be a meeting of your department in which you have to get up and explain some new company policy. It may be a retirement dinner for someone in your area of responsibility, and you're expected to make a "few appropriate remarks." I've seen managers go to unbelievable lengths to avoid such speaking situations, such as arranging a business trip so they'll be out of town, or scheduling their own vacation for that time. They'll spend the rest of their business lives plotting how not to get up in front of a group and speak. How much better off they'd be if they'd obtain the necessary skills and turn these negative situations into a resounding plus.

What many people don't realize is that learning to be an adequate public speaker will also improve their ability to speak extemporaneously. How do you respond when you're unexpectedly called on to say a few words? The most extreme example of someone who has difficulty in front of an audience is the person "who couldn't lead a group in silent prayer."

The close friend who first got me interested in public speaking is fond of saying, "Speech training won't get rid of the butterflies in your stomach, but it will organize them into effective squadrons."

Toastmasters International

It seems appropriate at this point to mention a nonprofit organization that I believe will help you learn how to be a capable public speaker. I'm referring to Toastmasters International, a self-help organization dedicated to the concept of developing skills in listening, thinking, and speaking. There are neither professionals nor staff members in these clubs, but only people with a mutual interest in developing their speaking capacity. For a modest semiannual fee, you receive the manuals you'll need to begin the process. You go at your own speed, and you'll find a group of people who help one another, not only by providing an audience, but also by engaging in formal evaluation sessions.

Another aspect of the Toastmaster training that I think is invaluable is what is called "Table Topics." This part of the meeting is designed to develop your skills in extemporaneous speaking. The Topic-Master calls on various people (usually those not scheduled to give a formal speech that evening) to talk for two or three minutes on a surprise subject. The time you have to prepare extends from the moment you rise from your chair until the moment you arrive at the lectern.

There are Toastmaster Clubs all over the world, so it's likely that you'll find one in your area. If not, you can write to get information about a club close to you. The world headquarters address is Toastmasters International, 2200 N. Grand Avenue, Santa Ana, California 92711.

Obviously, since these clubs include all kinds of individuals, you'll find degrees of quality. But you'll probably gain benefit in direct proportion to the effort you put into it. Most of these clubs meet weekly. Some are dinner clubs and some are not. Naturally, the dinner clubs will cost you more money each week.

There are other ways to get speech training. My recommendation of Toastmasters does not exclude other organizations that can help you get the job done. For example, certain community colleges offer public speaking training. Your desire to obtain these skills is the most important ingredient. Most of the people in your company will be too lazy to go out and do it. They'd then have to get off their butt and away from the TV set one night each week. They'd like to be a smooth public speaker if they could swallow a vitamin pill once a week, but if it's going to require any effort—forget it.

Fringe Benefits

How many outstanding public speakers do you personally know, either inside or outside your organization? I'll bet not many, if any. Why don't you resolve to be one of the few who is outstanding? Think of the possibilities, not only for promotion within your company, but for positions of leadership within the community. As a matter of fact, the opportunities for leadership challenges may come more quickly outside the company. Consider what that may open up for you. There are a lot of followers out there waiting for someone to lead them. One characteristic most outstanding leaders have is the ability to speak persuasively on public occasions. There's no reason why you can't be one of those few leaders. You don't have to be brighter than everyone else. There'll always be someone with more smarts than you, but it won't do him or her as much good if you excel in your ability to communicate.

Conclusion

We've covered a variety of topics in this book on how to lead people. We certainly haven't covered every situation you'll confront in your career as a manager—or even within the first few weeks in your new role.

There's no way that a book of this sort can be made all-inclusive. I can only hope that I've given you some insight into the techniques of managing people that will make the job more meaningful and understandable. You may think that I've spent an inordinate amount of time on attitudes, on how you view yourself and the problems you face, but that's exactly where your success or failure in working with people will be determined—in your head.

If you're the type of person who believes you're primarily controlled by events, then what's the use? You're then merely a puppet with some giant puppet master pulling the strings. But in actuality it's not that way. Although events beyond your control do have an impact on your life, you control how and what you think. That in turn controls your reaction to these events.

I haven't conned you in this book. I haven't told you that if you work hard and keep your nose clean you'll rise to the top. However, I do think you'll have a better chance if you follow some of these concepts than if you ignore what to me are basic truths. You didn't come into this world with any guarantee that everything would be fair and that the deserving would always get what they deserve. They don't! However, you obviously have no chance to achieve your goals if you just sit there and wait for lightning to strike.

We must grow. This book is devoted to exploring how you manage your people, but I'm just as interested in seeing you grow as a total person. I believe your career can add to your total growth, since it's such a large part of your life. We shouldn't work at a job we don't like, but on the other hand we must be realistic in recognizing that all careers contain aspects we don't like. It's the balance that's important. If most of the job is enjoyable, ego-satisfying, and challenging, then you can put up with the few parts you don't care for. If it's the other way around and you dislike most of what you have to do, you've obviously in the wrong career and you ought to change it. Life is too short to spend in a career that destroys you.

Perhaps Abraham Lincoln was right when he said, "Most people are about as happy as they make up their minds to be." That summarizes what I've tried to say throughout this book about the primacy of attitude.

Too many people, as they approach their middle years, start thinking in terms of the kind of contribution they're making to the world. They often become depressed because they believe what they're doing is not very important. They ask themselves, "How significant is it that I'm a manager in a company making bolts?" Put in that context, it may not seem terribly relevant. But the question that should be asked is, "What kind of impact am I having on the people I come in contact with, both in my work and in my personal life?"

If you can answer that question in a positive way, then it doesn't matter if the company you're associated with is making bolts or distributing fertilizer. The system isn't the payoff; the product isn't the payoff; your impact on the people whose lives you touch is what's important. Also, holding a position that's a little higher on the organization chart *does not* make you more important than they are. An executive or a manager is a combination of leader and servant. Not many executives are willing to accept the servant aspect of their responsibilities, because it interferes with their exalted opinion of their rank.

In developing systems for your people to use, you're in fact serving them. In maintaining a salary administration and performance appraisal system, you're serving them. In working out vacation schedules that will allow your people to maximize the benefits of their relaxation time, you're serving them. In hiring and training quality people for your department, you're serving the people who are already there.

Most people have no difficulty understanding the concept that the President of the United States has immense power but is also a servant. The same—"writ small"—applies to managerial jobs. There's a combination of what appear to be contradictory concepts: authority and a responsibility to serve. If you can keep these in some semblance of balance, I think you'll avoid getting an inflated view of your own importance and you'll do a better job.

You don't necessarily get smarter. You become more experienced, which many people mistake for wisdom but it doesn't matter what it's called as long as you continually become more effective. You become more effective as you develop a greater variety of experience in working with people. You gain little from repeating the same experiences except a smoothness that might not otherwise develop.

And the point, although elementary, bears repetition: There's a great deal to be gained from developing empathy for your subordinates' attitudes and feelings. Can you really sense how you'd want to be treated if you were in their position?

I truly wish the best for you as you direct people in what amounts to nearly one-half of their waking hours. Your success as a manager starts with you and your attitude toward that responsibility. If this book has been of some help to you, then its author is deeply gratified.

PERFORMANCE APPRAISAL

Name of employee _____ Job title _____

Department, division, unit _____

Date of employment _____ Date to current position _____

Period of rating _____ to _____ Date of appraisal _____

Person doing appraisal _____

Person reviewing appraisal _____

(Place an "x" in the appropriate blank)

Volume of work
- −10 ——— Cannot keep up with required volume.
- − 5 ——— Not up to requirements. Improvement necessary.
- 0 ——— Satisfactory production.
- + 5 ——— Consistently better than required.
- +10 ——— Clearly outstanding.

Work quality
- −10 ——— Work is far below requirements. Many errors.
- − 5 ——— Not up to requirements. Improvement necessary.
- 0 ——— Satisfactory quality.
- + 5 ——— Occasional errors. Usually accurate.
- +10 ——— Virtually mistake-free performance.

Attitude
- −10 ——— Apparently does not care; needs tight supervision.
- − 5 ——— Attitude mixed, not consistent.
- 0 ——— Satisfactory attitude.
- + 5 ——— Applies self well, requires occasional supervision.
- +10 ——— Completely self-reliant, requires direction only.

Job understanding
- −10 ——— Does not understand the job.
- − 5 ——— Some knowledge. Improvement necessary.
- 0 ——— Satisfactory job understanding and knowledge.
- + 5 ——— Understands job well.
- +10 ——— Outstanding knowledge of job and its integration with company objectives.

Comprehension ability	−10 ——	Does not grasp instructions. Must be constantly shown routine.
	− 5 ——	Understands instructions slowly, but does retain them once mastered.
	0 ——	Satisfactory grasp of new ideas.
	+ 5 ——	Learns quickly and retains what is learned.
	+10 ——	Exceptionally quick to comprehend. Retains instructions and concepts.

Attendance	−10 ——	Absent or late often.
	− 5 ——	Absent or late slightly beyond acceptable limits.
	0 ——	Satisfactory.
	+ 5 ——	Occasional absence.
	+10 ——	Seldom absent and seldom late.

ADD NUMBERS NEXT TO BLANK CHECKED

−50	——	Unacceptable performance. (Rating not applicable to new employee.)
−25 to −50	——	Unsatisfactory; improvement imperative.
−10 to −25	——	Needs improvement.
0	——	Satisfactory.
+10 to +25	——	Seasoned performance.
+25 to +50	——	Outstanding performance.
+50	——	Superior performance; beyond expectations.

ADDITIONAL COMMENTS: